STANDARDIZED
SURVEY
INTERVIEWING

Applied Social Research Methods Series
Volume 18

APPLIED SOCIAL RESEARCH
METHODS SERIES

Series Editor:
LEONARD BICKMAN, Peabody College, Vanderbilt University
Series Associate Editor:
DEBRA ROG, National Institute of Mental Health

This series is designed to provide students and practicing professionals in the social sciences with relatively inexpensive softcover textbooks describing the major methods used in applied social research. Each text introduces the reader to the state of the art of that particular method and follows step-by-step procedures in its explanation. Each author describes the theory underlying the method to help the student understand the reasons for undertaking certain tasks. Current research is used to support the author's approach.

STANDARDIZED SURVEY INTERVIEWING

Minimizing Interviewer-Related Error

Floyd J. Fowler, Jr.
Thomas W. Mangione

Applied Social Research Methods Series
Volume 18

SAGE PUBLICATIONS
The Publishers of Professional Social Science
Newbury Park   London   New Delhi

For information address:

SAGE Publications, Inc.
2111 West Hillcrest Drive
Newbury Park, California 91320

SAGE Publications Ltd.
28 Banner Street
London EC1Y 8QE
England

SAGE Publications India Pvt. Ltd.
M-32 Market
Greater Kailash I
New Delhi 110 048 India

Printed in the United States of America

Library of Congress Cataloging-in-Publication Data

Fowler, Floyd J.
    Standardized survey interviewing ; minimizing interviewer-related
error / by Floyd J. Fowler, Jr. and Thomas W. Mangione.
        p. cm. — (Applied social research methods series ; 18)
    Bibliography: p.
    Includes index.
    ISBN 0-8039-3092-5. — ISBN 0-8039-3093-3 (pbk.)
    1. Interviewing. 2. Social sciences — Research. 3. Social
surveys. I. Mangione, Thomas W. II. Title. III. Series: Applied
social research methods series ; v. 18.
H61.28.F68   1990
300'.723—dc20   89-10514
                                                             CIP

FIRST PRINTING, 1990

CONTENTS

TABLES

FOREWORD

In the last 35 years, since Herbert Hyman and associates wrote a landmark book about survey interviewers, social scientists have learned quite a bit about how interviewers contribute to error in survey data. Although interviewers have not been a "hot" topic in methodological research since 1954, there has been a growing body of knowledge we felt should be summarized.

We know that interviewers affect the answers they are given in surveys. We also know that there are strategies for reducing interviewer-related error but, to a great extent, those strategies are not common in survey research practice today. Our goals in writing this book include giving cost-effective advice about doing better surveys, and providing evidence to those who seek funding for surveys that justify the comparatively small expenditures that can make a big difference in the quality of survey data.

Obviously those directly involved in executing population surveys constitute a primary audience for this book. However, interviewers collect data for many research purposes. Anyone who is obtaining information from others that will be tabulated or put into quantitative form should be interested in ways to minimize interviewer-related error. Thus, this book is written with a broad audience in mind, and does not assume a background in research methods, statistics, or any particular discipline.

We are serious about the idea that survey research is a social science. We think measurement in the social sciences can be just as rigorous and valid as in any other of the sciences. We cringe when someone says interviewing or question design is an art, not a science. There are procedures that must be followed to maximize the validity of measurement in surveys just as there are in other scientific efforts. This book is a compendium of these procedures; it documents how interviewers affect data, and how to minimize those effects to produce more valid data.

The human part of surveys is problematic to users of survey data. Some critics think consistent, standardized interviews are impossible; other users of survey data think standardization is a given and take it for granted. Neither is true. Measurement through interviewing is possible, but it is far from easy. It will not happen—at least not very well—if interviewing is not good. Interviewers and respondents are just people, and effective measurement procedures must take into account this reality. We hope we have done a good job of laying out what it takes to produce good interviewing under the realistic conditions under which interviews take place.

Here's to more of it!

—Floyd J. Fowler, Jr.
—Thomas W. Mangione

ACKNOWLEDGMENTS

The impetus for this book, and much of the data presented, came from a large-scale experiment to study the value of interviewer training and supervision. That project was funded by Grant # 3-R18-HS04189 from the National Center for Health Services Research.

The National Center for Health Services Research deserves credit for funding this effort. Health researchers spend an ever increasing amount of resources on collecting survey data. Information is needed that can only be provided by surveys. However, the amount spent on evaluating and designing survey methods is very small. There is a continuing need for investment in research methodology, and we are grateful that this work was chosen to be a part of NCHSR's overall program of health services research.

Two project monitors at NCHSR deserve our thanks for their time, effort and interest: Bill Kitching and Stephen Marcus.

Executing the experiment itself was a major achievement. Barbara Thomas, Alice Fehlhaber, Ruth Paradise, Kim Streitburger, and Dottie Cerankowski among many played particularly key roles in the management of that complex effort.

The statistical advice of Tom Louis, then at the Harvard School of Public Health, now at the University of Minnesota, was a very important resource.

We also want to acknowledge our special debt to Charles F. Cannell. The products of his research are cited continuously in this book, and his intellectual contributions go well beyond the citations. No one has done more to add to our understanding of interviewers.

We want to thank Anstis Benfield and Peggy Carter for typing this manuscript.

Various colleagues reviewed and contributed to the work reported here in various forms, and we are grateful for their help. However, of course, final responsibility for the data and conclusions presented here is solely the authors'.

1

What Is a Standardized Survey Interview?

This book is a product of continuing efforts to learn how to improve the quality of survey data. The surveys that are our particular concern are those designed to produce quantitative data about some population; for example, to estimate the percentage of the population that owns a car or was hospitalized in the previous year. The data are collected by asking questions of the people who are to be described. Although some surveys rely on self-administered techniques—having people answer written questions by filling out questionnaires—this book pertains to that large proportion of surveys that use interviewers to ask questions and to record the answers. The primary purpose of this book is to describe how to conduct such interviews to minimize the error that can be attributed to interviewers.

THE NATURE OF SURVEY INTERVIEWS

An interview has been described as a "conversation with a purpose" (e.g., Kahn and Cannell, 1958). However, there are many different types of interviews, and the specific purpose of the conversation affects which procedures are appropriate. Furthermore, the definition of success, the standards of quality if you will, also will vary depending on these distinct purposes.

A standardized survey interview constitutes only one of many types of interviews, but there are two essential components which are common to all types of interviews:

1. The substantive part of the conversation consists of questions and answers.
2. The participants have defined, non-overlapping roles: one person asks the questions (the interviewer) and the other answers the questions (the respondent).

In categorizing some conversations as interviews, the presence of highly differentiated roles is a crucial element. Although an interviewer may volunteer information or explanations, this behavior is only to prepare for the question asking event. Likewise, although a respondent may ask questions of the interviewer, these are in pursuit of succeeding at the answering process.

There are several features of survey interviews designed to provide descriptive statistics about a population that distinguish them from interviews conducted for other reasons:

1. The individual respondents are of interest only because they are members of the population to be described. Typically, they are part of a representative sample of that population. Regardless of how they were chosen, the answers of individuals are of interest because they will help the researcher describe the population from which they were drawn, not because there is any intrinsic interest in the answers of these individuals per se.

2. The product of the survey will be a quantitative or mathematical description of the population. At the very least, the researcher will be interested in sorting respondents into discrete, well-defined categories and estimating the percentage of the population that falls into those categories. A typical product of a survey is a statement such as, "4% of the labor force is currently unemployed." Descriptions may also identify relationships among characteristics such as: "Workers who are dissatisfied with their jobs take more sick leave days than workers who are satisfied."

3. The results of the measurement process, the data to be analyzed, are the answers given by the respondents. The descriptions are a direct result of the distribution of respondents who gave particular types of answers.

The standard for the success of a survey is how well the data measures the aspects of the population the researchers are trying to describe. The goal of a survey is to produce accurate statistics.

SOURCES OF ERROR IN SURVEYS

A survey is a series of steps that together form a measurement process. To evaluate the quality of estimates based on a survey, each aspect of the survey process should be considered:

1. Any survey estimate based on a sample is subject to sampling error, error stemming from the fact that by chance a sample may not be exactly the same in all respects as the population from which it was drawn. The way a sample is selected, as well as its size, affects how well a sample is likely to represent a population. Moreover, survey estimates are based on those actually answering the questions. Some selected people usually refuse to be interviewed or are not interviewed for other reasons. The rate at which data are obtained from sampled persons, and the extent to which those answering are representative, is another critical issue in evaluating survey data.

2. Questions vary greatly in how accurately they are answered. The kinds of information sought in a survey, and the wording of the specific questions, have a direct effect on the quality of answers to surveys.

3. The procedures used to collect data also matter. Whether data collection occurs by telephone or in person, the context of the interview, and the way the interviewer handles the interaction with the respondent all can influence the amount and types of errors in survey estimates.

4. The process of putting survey answers into numerical form for computer analysis may contribute to error. In the coding process, inconsistency is introduced if coders differ in the way they apply coding rules or if they use faulty judgment when working with the codes. Also, data entry errors can contribute to the overall error found in surveys.

These sources of error in surveys are summarized in Table 1.1.

THE ROLE OF THE INTERVIEWER

Of the sources of error outlined in Table 1.1, most are not the responsibility of interviewers. Surveys usually are carried out by a team of workers. One individual, or set of individuals (the "researchers"), makes the design decisions: the objectives, the sample design, the specific questions to be asked, and the data collection procedures to be used. Typically, another set of individuals is responsible for actually carrying out the data collection. Although in some small surveys researchers may do all or some of the interviewing, and/or only a single interviewer is used, a critical feature of most surveys is that researchers have to design data collection procedures that many other people will carry out.

Interviewers do affect the response rate, the percentage of sampled people who agree to be interviewed. However, the error in surveys that is attributable to interviewers stems mainly from their influence on the way they and their respondents handle the data collection process. More specifically, it is when interviewers fail to be standardized that they are responsible for error. The challenge for researchers and interviewers, working together, is to bring standardization to the interviewing process.

SURVEY AS MEASUREMENT:
THE NEED FOR STANDARDIZATION

According to Webster's dictionary (Guralk, 1976) to measure is "to find out or estimate the extent, dimensions, etc. (of anything) by a standard."

Table 1.1

Sources of Error in Surveys

A. The Samples Are a Source of Error:
 1. When the sampling frame, or list from which the sample was selected does not include everyone in the population to be described, thereby leaving some types of people out of the sample;
 2. Because there is some probability that by chance alone a sample will not perfectly reflect the population from which it was drawn; and
 3. When those selected to be in the sample do not provide answers either by refusing to participate altogether or by selectively refusing to provide answers to specific questions.

B. Questions Are Sources of Error:
 1. When they are misunderstood;
 2. When they require information that respondents do not have or cannot recall accurately; and
 3. When respondents are not willing to answer accurately.

C. Interviewers Are a Source of Error:
 1. When they do not read questions as worded;
 2. When they probe directively;
 3. When they bias answers by the way they relate to respondents; and
 4. When they record answers inaccurately.

D. Data Reduction Is a Source of Error:
 1. When coders inconsistently apply coding rules or use faulty judgement about the appropriate codes to apply; and
 2. When data are entered incorrectly into computer-usable files.

The key defining part of a measurement process is standardization. In all sciences, meaningful measurement occurs by applying the same procedure across a set of situations so that differences in the readings that result can be compared and interpreted as indicating real differences in what is being measured. The same is true for surveys. In this case, though, the standardized measurement process is asking a question and the "measurement" that comes out of the process is the respondent's answer as recorded by an interviewer. The goal of standardization is that each respondent be exposed to the same question experience, and that the recording of answers be the same, too, so that any differences in the answers can be correctly interpreted as reflecting differences between respondents rather than differences in the process that produced the answer.

It is easy to say interviewers should be standardized; it is not so easy to accomplish. To clarify the issues, we need an example:

QUESTION: "How would you rate the school that your oldest child attends—very good, good, fair, or poor?"

RESPONDENT: "That is complicated for me. My child is in the second grade, I do not think they are doing a very good job in areas such as numbers and reading skills. However, at this age, I do not think that the content of what they learn is all that important. Kids can catch up in that respect. On the other hand, I think they do an excellent job in recreational areas such as gym and recess, where there is good equipment and a lot of opportunities for the kids to do things together. I think that is very important at this age."

ANALYSIS: This respondent has a legitimate problem with the question. Schools have many facets: physical plants, teachers, administration, curricula, and other students. A question such as this forces respondents to take into account all the various aspects of a school and somehow put the pieces together in a way that makes sense to produce a single rating. Interviewers can respond to an answer such as this in either a nonstandardized or standardized fashion.

Nonstandardized Interviewer Response Option Number 1: "When we are asking about schools, I think the educational component is probably what schools are mainly about. I think you should give your rating in terms of the educational programs at the school."

Nonstandardized Interviewer Response Option Number 2: "You are being asked to rate a school as a whole. It would make sense to give the greatest weight to the aspects of the school that you value most."

Standardized Interviewer Response: "Obviously there are many things that go into how you feel about a school. The way a survey works is to ask people the same questions and let them interpret and answer each question in a way that seems best to them. Let me read you the question again, and you give me the answer which from your perspective is the best answer to this question as it is written."

Further Analysis: It is safe to assume that some respondents will answer the question the way the first nonstandardized response suggested while others will adopt a frame of reference suggested by nonstandardized response number 2. The point is that which frame of reference is adopted will be affected by the interviewer if one of the nonstandardized probes or explanations is adopted. If the interviewer behaves in a standardized way, we will not know which approach was taken by the respondent (unless another question is asked), but we will know that differences in the answers stem from the way the respondent interpreted and answered the question, not from the way the interviewer behaved. That is what we are after.

RESPONDENT: "I think the most accurate answer is that in some ways I think the school is pretty good and in others it is not very good."

ANALYSIS: The respondent has given a thoughtful, accurate answer, but it will be impossible to integrate that answer with the answers of other respondents to produce quantitative descriptions. Although some survey questions call for all respondents to answer in their own words (called open-ended or narrative answers), many questions, like this one, ask respondents to choose the one answer from a list of answers that best describes their feelings or situation. Specifying the form the answer is to take is part of standardization.

Standardized Interviewer Response: "I need to have you pick just one answer so we can compare your answers with those of other respondents. Which of these answers best summarizes your overall rating of the school—very good, good, fair, or poor?"

It obviously would be easier to accept a qualified answer, rather than forcing the respondent to respond by choosing one answer from alternatives that may not fit his or her feelings very well. It also would be easier and more natural for the interviewer to help the respondent by using non-standardized clarifications. However, these procedures are necessary if measurement is to be consistent across interviews, and they are key parts of what we mean by a standardized interview.

A COMPARISON WITH TWO OTHER TYPES OF INTERVIEWS

To help provide perspective on the specialized requirements for standardized interviewing, we will compare a standardized survey interview with:

A. an interview on a late night talk show; and
B. a physician interviewing a patient about his or her medical history.

On the surface, it may seem silly to compare an interview on a talk show with a standardized survey interview. However, such interviews do meet the minimum criteria of having questions and answers as the main focus of the conversation and having role differentiation between the participants, with one person mainly asking the questions and one person mainly answering.

The most fundamental difference is that the purpose of the interaction on the talk show is entertainment. The answers will not be used for any purpose after the interaction is over; indeed, no one writes them down.

The questions may be predesigned and structured, but they bear little or no relationship to the questions any other guest on the show will be asked. Some interviewers will attempt to "bring out" their guests, giving them chances to express themselves fully and completely and trying not to impose their own personalities on the interactions. Although those tend to be characteristics of what we consider to be a "good" interviewer, some hosts also use the questions as opportunities to be entertaining in their own right, sometimes cutting off the guests' communication efforts. From the point of view of entertainment value, such a process may be as successful as when the host behaves as a "good" interviewer.

Finally, the focus of a talk-show interview is only on one particular guest at a time. There is no effort to quantify. There is no reason to compare one set of answers with the answers that anyone else gives. No further use will be made of the results of this interview, except possibly reruns or anniversary shows.

When a physician interviews a patient for the first time about his or her medical history, the structure of the interaction looks very much like a survey interview. There is no ambiguity about who is asking the questions and who is answering them. Moreover, physicians typically work from a list of conditions and past medical events that they use for virtually all patients.

There are several differences between a physician interview of patients and a standardized survey interview, however. First, the goal is to characterize correctly the particular individual patient. There is no interest in generalizing to other patients, nor will there be any effort to compare the results for one patient with other patients. Hence, the wording of questions is likely to vary from patient to patient. While the physician may start out with the same protocol for all patients, he or she will also feel free to digress and explore idiosyncratic avenues of inquiry if answers given by the respondent seem to warrant it.

Moreover, most physicians are not concerned about being nondirective. It is not uncommon for physicians to suggest words to describe respondent feelings so that they can translate respondent experiences into a medical framework. The results or products of the medical history are not the words or answers the respondents give themselves but rather the conclusions that the physician reaches on the basis of the answers respondents give. Thus, if the patient says he has "heart trouble," the physician will take that information into account, but the medical conclusion of the physician will be based on his/her judgment. For the most part, the data recorded as a result of the medical history interview also are the physician's conclusions rather than the answers the patient gives per se.

Table 1.2

Comparison of Types of Interviews

Type	Quantitative goals	Use of answers	Standardization of questions
Talk show	none	entertainment	none
Medical history	match patients to condition profiles	provide information for diagnosis	same general topics but not same questions
Standardized survey	describe population	become the data to be analyzed	identical questions across all interviews

In fact the interviewers in most situations could probably do well by applying some of the principles of standardized, non-directive interviewing. The talk show host will have a more interesting and diverse program if the interviews are respondent oriented, with a minimum of intrusion of the views and predilections of the interviewer. Physicians, too, could benefit from a standardized interviewing approach. Because physicians know that their conclusions, not what the patients say per se, are the important products of the interview, physician interviewers may develop directive interviewing techniques, which have patients agreeing with physician statements that in fact do not quite capture what they are experiencing. Physician conclusions are the critical product, but such conclusions are most accurate and valid if they take full advantage of what information patients can provide.

A standardized survey interview is indeed a very special instance of that form of interaction called an interview. However, the challenges of a standardized interview, to have respondents answer questions accurately and completely and to minimize the effect of the interviewer on the answers, apply to most interview situations. The procedures and techniques required to produce standardization in surveys that involve a large number of interviewers across a wide range of respondents pose a special challenge, but the procedures and the solutions that work in standardized surveys have wide applicability to other types of interviewing.

WHEN AND WHEN NOT TO STANDARDIZE IN SOCIAL RESEARCH

When one is collecting information for social research, a standardized interview is not always appropriate.

Exploratory research usually is not done best using standardized interviews. By design, in a standardized interview one only learns the answers to the questions that are asked. At the exploratory stages of research, finding out which questions to ask is a major goal. Also restricting or structuring answers is good practice in standardized interviews, but it should not be done until the researcher is sure the answer options are comprehensive and appropriate.

Case studies, when the research goal is to describe fully a set of individuals or organizations, also may require less standardized interviewing techniques. A typical approach for such studies is to enlist respondents as collaborators in the research, explaining to them what is wanted and asking them to provide the needed information. The specific areas to be covered are specified, but follow-up questions are used freely to obtain further explanations on topics about which the interviewer wants more information.

In a related way, some social research interviews are used to study characteristics of individuals that cannot be measured by respondent answers per se. Narrative answers are analyzed and conclusions are reached about the respondents that respondents could not articulate themselves (Mishler, 1986). For example, respondents might be asked to describe how they responded to some stressful situations, and the researchers might then code whether the coping styles were "constructive" or "destructive" from the point of view of solving problems.

In such research studies, investigators do not look at the interview as measurement but rather as information gathering. Interviewers typically will explain and clarify questions, ask new questions, and record summaries of the answers they are given, all forbidden activities in a standardized interview. To try to produce some consistency in such interviews, usually a comparatively small number of interviewers are used who are thoroughly immersed in the research objectives. Even then, researchers can run into problems when they want to compare answers unless they are sure people were answering the same questions and responding within a consistent framework. For that reason, including some standardized questions in less standardized interviews is often very helpful. However, the point is that there are legitimate research goals that involve interviews that are not standardized.

On the other hand, there also are criticisms that may appear to pertain to standardized interviews that, in fact, seem to us to be aimed at some other issue. For example, standardized surveys usually rely heavily on closed or fixed-response questions. Some researchers prefer narrative responses to fixed-alternative questions (e.g., Mishler, 1986). Open-ended or narrative answers do tell researchers more about what is going on in the mind of the respondent; however, they do not provide information which is as amenable to quantitative analysis as do the closed-response answers.

Moreover, asking questions that are answered in a narrative form does not in any way preclude standardized administration of an interview. The same generalizations about interpretability of answers apply whether the questions were asked in an open or closed format. We think both kinds of questions are valuable and both should be handled in a standardized way when the goal is to produce quantitative data.

Another issue is the importance of standardization for gathering factual or objective information. There is little debate among researchers that answers about subjective states, opinions, feelings, or perceptions, are highly dependent on the details of question wording. However, some people might argue that standardized questions are not so important for gathering factual information such as the number of visits to doctors, the number of hospitalizations, or the age of household members. Yet even the simplest question requires that respondents all share the same understanding of terms and concepts. Hence, when respondents are supposed to report their annual incomes, it is important that everyone share an understanding of which sources of income count, and which do not, and for what period of time income is to be reported. Hence, giving all respondents the same, complete definition of terms will help ensure that the researcher gets what is desired and has obtained the same information from everyone.

However, the most critical issue of debate about standardization focuses on what an interviewer should do when a respondent encounters trouble with a question. Clearly, it is not possible to construct questions that are always clear and mean the same thing to all respondents. If a respondent is uncertain about the meaning of a term or what is wanted by a question, should an interviewer explain, clarify, and rephrase the question or should the interviewer leave it up to the respondent to decide what the question means? This is probably the sharpest area of controversy between those who insist on standardization and those who encourage interviewer innovation to solve respondent problems (Mishler, 1986).

Our most important point is that to the extent that respondents do not understand questions consistently, there is going to be a problem with the measurement no matter what the interviewer does or does not do. We believe there is nothing that an interviewer can do to produce good measurement when given a bad question. The time to deal with bad questions is before a survey is fielded, not during the interview process once the survey is underway.

Consider again the example above in which a respondent was asked to rate the quality of his or her child's school. Let us say that the researcher actually wanted respondents to rate the school from an educational vantage point, but neglected to state it in the question. Hence, in our example, some respondents might consider the physical facilities or the physical education program in making their ratings. If a respondent appears to misunderstand the question, based on some comment about it, or if the respondent asks the interviewer about the meaning of the question, some would say the interviewer should clarify what the researcher intended. We think that is counterproductive and will lead to worse measurement, not better.

1. If interviewers are free to change or amend questions when they sense respondent uncertainty or confusion, in essence some respondents will be asked one question and another set of respondents will be asked another question, and no one will be sure at the time of analysis who answered what question. Moreover, it is inappropriate to combine or compare answers when, in effect, respondents answered different questions.

2. Unless a single researcher is doing all the interviewing, or unless there is only an extremely small team of interviewers, we think it is highly unlikely that interviewers will provide consistent help in problem solving to respondents when they are asked to provide definitions or explanations that go beyond the questions. We are convinced that, in fact, when given that kind of discretion, interviewers will create as many answers that are not consistent with the researchers' goals as they will answers that improve the quality of data and make them more consistent with researchers' goals.

There are many appropriate ways to use interviews in social science research, and only a subset of those require standardized interviewing. However, when the goal is to produce quantitative data, we think that a standardized, nondirective interview is what is needed.

ABOUT THE BOOK:
APPROACHES TO MINIMIZING INTERVIEWER-RELATED ERROR

The main goals of this book are to describe how interviewer characteristics and behavior affect the quality of survey data, and the strategies available to researchers to reduce interviewer-related error in survey measurement. The principles discussed apply whether interviews are done in person or over the telephone, though more research is needed to clarify the implications of mode of data collection for how interviewers should behave.

A book about ways to reduce or control interviewer-related error requires an understanding of the nature of that error. Chapter 2 contains a discussion of the nature of interviewer-related error and how to measure it.

All survey organizations acknowledge the importance of the way the interviewer handles the question-and-answer process in producing standardized interviewing. A set of standards for asking questions, probing incomplete answers, and recording answers has evolved. Those procedures are described in Chapter 3.

In an interview, the question-and-answer process itself is, in a sense, a play within a play. It is a structured interaction within some broader context that brings the interviewer and respondent together. Moreover, in the most prevalent sorts of surveys, the interviewer calls the respondent on the telephone, or visits his or her home, and establishes a relationship in which this interaction can occur. With virtually no background or history to the relationship, using an advance letter at most, the interviewer engages in introductory, orienting behavior, then launches into the interview.

Relatively speaking, this aspect of the interview has been neglected. However, Charles Cannell and his associates have produced an extensive body of research over the past twenty years documenting the importance of the context within which the interview takes place for the quality of information produced. In particular, they have focussed on the way in which interviewers handle the orientation of the respondent to establish the interview context. In Chapter 4, what is now known about the context of the interviewer-respondent interaction and how that affects the quality of survey data is presented.

Perhaps the first step taken by researchers to improve the quality of survey measurement was to give interviewers a script. In the early days of survey studies, interviewers were sent out only with a set of objectives and instructions to collect information from people on specific topics (Converse, 1987). It was soon learned that different interviewers asked different questions, which in turn had an important influence on the answers that came back. Researchers learned that if they wrote down the questions to be asked, so that the interviewers all asked the same questions, the effect of interviewers on the resulting answers was much reduced. Even though the basic insight that interviewers should all ask the same questions has been accepted for more than fifty years, it still turns out that improving the design of questions may be the most important way to control interviewer-related error. Chapter 5 presents current knowledge about how to design survey questions to minimize interviewer-related error.

Anyone thinking about how to maximize the quality of interviewing would suggest using good interviewers. One of the more developed bodies of research on the interviewer is whether interviewer characteristics, such as religion, race, gender, age, or education produce errors in the answers obtained. The way interviewers are trained and the kind of supervision they receive are also obvious candidates for affecting the way interviewers perform their jobs and the quality of data they collect. Chapters 6, 7, and 8 summarize the current state of knowledge about how the selection, training, and supervision of interviewers affects the quality of interviewing and the quality of survey estimates.

In the concluding chapter, Chapter 9, we provide a prescriptive summary based on established research of how to minimize interviewer-related error and maximize the quality of survey-based estimates by using standardized interviewing procedures.

2

`What Is Interviewer-Related Error?`

Measuring error in surveys is not easy. In theory, error is the difference between a survey answer and the "true value" of what the researcher wants to measure. For certain factual questions, such as respondent age or the number of visits to doctors, it may be possible to check the survey answer against a reliable record, but in practice such checks are seldom performed or even feasible. For questions about subjective phenomena, such as opinions, feelings, or perceptions, there does not exist even in theory a direct way to assess the accuracy of an answer.

In the absence of a direct assessment of error, methodologists measure error in a roundabout way. To the extent that they can observe variation in responses or differences in the average responses that could not reasonably reflect what they are trying to measure, they conclude that there is measurement error.

It is not controversial to posit that the characteristics or behavior of the measurer should not affect the results of a measurement. Hence, to the extent that interviewers can be associated with the answers they obtain, we know there is at least that much error in the measurement process. When we speak of interviewer-related error in this book, we are referring to variation in answers that can be associated with the people who did the interviews.

We also know there are many potential sources of error in survey data that are not related to the interviewer:

1. question wording can affect answers;
2. respondent characteristics unrelated to what is being measured can affect answers;
3. the setting in which an interview occurs can affect answers;
4. the position of a question in an interview schedule can affect answers; and
5. even the presence of any interviewer at all, as compared with having the respondent fill out a form, can affect answers.

When any feature of the data collection process affects the answers, error can be inferred. However, this book does not directly address these other sources of error. If interviewers are given a set of questions to ask and they do so in a way that individual interviewers do not affect the answers, for our purposes there is no interviewer-related error. If the answers do not measure what they are intended to measure, the solution lies in better questions or better procedures, not in better interviewing. This book is only about minimizing the error, the variation in responses, that results from interviewer characteristics and how the interviewer performs the job.

THE SIGNIFICANCE OF STANDARDIZATION

Given the way we are defining interviewer-related error, it is tautological to say that standardized interviewing is the way to reduce it. The test of whether or not interviewers are standardized is whether or not they affect the answers. If interviewers can be shown to affect answers, they are not standardized; if they do not affect answers, they are standardized.

There is a host of empirical questions, however, about what interviewer behaviors and procedures are most effective in producing a consistent data collection process. Obviously, in real settings, we cannot make interviewer behavior the same in every way, and our critical task is to identify ways to minimize the differences between interviewers that actually affect answers. To that end, we outline a variety of procedures and techniques designed to maximize the consistency of interviewing, but the test of the efficacy of these solutions lies in assessments of whether or not interviewers are affecting answers.

It is important for readers to have a sense of what interviewer effects do to data, because they reduce the ability of researchers to reach valid conclusions. There are two perspectives on interviewer effects on data. Both are valid, though one comes from the psychometric approach to measurement and the other from the sampling statisticians' approach to measurement.

The psychometric approach is the one that was implicit in the introduction to this chapter. The two common standards for the quality of measurement in the social sciences are reliability and validity. Reliability of a measurement is the extent to which it produces consistent results; if one is measuring the same characteristic or situation repeatedly, the results should be the same. To the extent that interviewers influence answers differentially across respondents or among themselves, inconsistency of measurement is a result. The answers obtained reflect not only the true value of what is being measured and whatever response idiosyncrasies the respondent brings to the situation, but also the effect of the interviewer on the answer. Obviously, the interviewer-induced component of the answer varies independently of what is being measured, resulting in unreliable data. Table 2.1 is a simplified summary of that model.

Table 2.1
Components of Variance of Answers

True Answer
+
Error Related to Interviewer
+
Response Error from Other Sources
=
Recorded Answer

Validity is the term used in the social sciences for the extent to which a measure actually corresponds with what the researcher is trying to measure. In theory, a survey measure's validity could be assessed by the correlation or correspondence between a survey answer and some error-free measure of the same thing. Hence, the correlation between a survey answer and some other measure of the same or a related phenomenon is likely to be the standard by which validity is assessed (Cronbach and Meehl, 1955).

Table 2.2 provides the equations and a summary of the relationship between interviewer-related error and reliability and validity. The simple fact is that to the extent that answers are affected by interviewers, to the extent that there is interviewer-related error, the correlation between the survey answers and what the researchers are trying to measure will be reduced; that is the operational indicator of validity, and it is one critical criterion for how well the measurement process has been carried out.

Sampling statisticians think about error in surveys in a somewhat different way. Rather than focusing on correlations between an answer and some criterion for its validity, sampling statisticians think about the precision of survey-based estimates such as means or proportions. There are two concerns. The first is bias, the extent to which the answers across all interviewers on average are different from the true value for the population. The second is precision, how close an estimate, such as a mean, based on one survey is likely to be to the estimate one would get if one did repeated surveys of the same population or if no sampling at all was involved (i.e., data were collected from everyone). Statisticians call this measure of precision the "standard error" of an estimate.

The bias in estimates is not indicative of a lack of standardization of interviewers. Making interviewers more consistent normally will not reduce

Table 2.2

The Effect of Unreliability on Correlations

1. OBSERVED VARIANCE (X) = TRUE VARIANCE (X) + ERROR VARIANCE (X)

   The variance of a measure has two components; the true variance and additional variance caused by unreliable measurement.

2. RELIABILITY = $1 - (\sqrt{\text{ERROR VARIANCE}} \: / \: \sqrt{\text{OBSERVED VARIANCE}})$

   The reliability of a measure is calculated by subtracting the ratio of the error variance divided by the total observed variance and subtracting this quantity (always less than 1.0) from 1. This gives a reliability coefficient that ranges from 1.0 to 0.0.

3. CORRELATION BETWEEN "X" AND "Y" =
   $$\text{TRUE CORRELATION} \times \sqrt{\text{RELIABILITY(x)} \times \text{RELIABILITY (y)}}$$

   The correlation between two measures is reduced in size by a factor which is the product of the square roots of the reliabilities of each of the measures.

4. VALIDITY(y) = CORRELATION BETWEEN "y" AND A CRITERION "x"

   The validity of a measure is determined by its correlation with a criterion variable.

THEREFORE: Interviewer induced error lowers the reliability of a measure which in turn limits its ability to reflect valid relationships.

average bias, and for the most part, this book is not about reduction of bias in survey estimates.

Unstandardized interviewing is important to sampling statisticians primarily because it increases the standard error of estimates. The more interviewers affect answers, the greater the standard errors for a particular sample.

To do research on interviewers, a statistic is needed that will tell us how much the interviewers are influencing the data. For this purpose, Kish (1962) proposed the intraclass correlation coefficient, which reflects how much of the variance in an estimate such as a mean, is associated with the interviewers. Since interviewers who are perfectly standardized should not be associated with the answers they obtain, an intraclass correlation of "zero" means that there are no interviewer effects. A nonzero coefficient indicates that interviewers are associated with answers.

The intraclass correlation is typically referred to as *rho*. It is a measure of interviewer effects that is independent of the number of interviews taken by each interviewer. For that reason, it can be used to compare interviewer effects by different groups of interviewers and by interviewers for different surveys. It also can be used to compare the extent to which different questions are affected by interviewers.

Real limits to the widespread use of *rho* include the fact that it can only be calculated if assignments of respondents to interviewers are representative subsamples of the whole sample and that formulas for computing *rho* are complicated.

Table 2.3 presents the formulas for calculating *rho* in the simplest situation. As the first equation shows, *rho* is the proportion of the total variance of an estimate such as a mean that is attributable to the interviewers. The figure also shows how to calculate an estimate of *rho* from the output from a standard analysis of variance if the underlying assumptions are met.

Typical significant values of *rho* are in the range of .01 to .02 (though sometimes they go as high as .10). Such values mean that one or two percent of the variance of such estimates can be attributable to the interviewers. Now, on the surface, such values would not seem to constitute a big problem. The key, however, is that this effect is multiplied by the number of

Table 2.3

Calculation of *Rho* and Design Effects

A. Conceptually *rho* is that proportion of the total variance of an estimate such as a mean that is associated with the interviewer.

$$\text{RHO} = \frac{\text{Variance (interviewer)}}{\text{Sampling variance} + \text{Variance (interviewer)}}$$

B. Using the output from an analysis of variance with interviewer as the random effects variable, *rho* can be calculated using the model mean square term and the error mean square term and the average number of interviews per interviewer.

$$\text{RHO*} = \frac{\text{Model MS} - \text{Error MS}}{\text{Model MS} + (n - 1)(\text{Error MS})}$$

C. The DEFT (the square root of the "design effect") is the inflation of the standard error above and beyond that due to sampling the population resulting from the fact that interviewers affect answers. Its value is dependent on the size of *rho* and the average number of interviews taken per interviewer.

$$\sqrt{\text{DESIGN EFFECT}} = \sqrt{1 + (n - 1)(\text{Rho})}$$
$$\text{(DEFT)}$$

*This calculation is only appropriate when certain conditions are met: 1) interviewers must interview a representative subsample of the total sample, and 2) the number of interviews taken per interviewer should be approximately equal. Readers are referred to Kish (1962), Stokes and Yeh (1988) and Groves and Magilavy (1980) for a fuller discussion of how to calculate *rho* and the assumptions on which calculations should be based.

Table 2.4

Multipliers of Estimates of Standard Errors of Means (DEFTS) Due to
Interviewer Effects* for Selected Values of
Rho and Average Interviewer Assignments

Average number of interviews per interviewer	*Intraclass correlation (Rho)*				
	.005	*.01*	*.015*	*.02*	*.03*
11	1.002	1.05	1.07	1.10	1.14
21	1.05	1.10	1.14	1.18	1.26
31	1.07	1.14	1.20	1.26	1.38
51	1.12	1.22	1.32	1.41	1.58
81	1.18	1.34	1.48	1.61	1.84
101	1.22	1.41	1.58	1.73	2.00

NOTE: *Estimates of standard errors calculated from the sample size and design should be inflated by the multiplier in the table to take into account the effect of interviewers.

respondents each interviewer interviews. As interviewers take more interviews, their impact on the data becomes more noticeable and significant.

There is a statistic called the design effect which provides a numerical representation of this effect; it is common to report the square root, usually referred to as *deft*. The bottom of Table 2.3 shows the formula for calculating *deft*, which is a function of the value of *rho* and the average number of interviews taken per interviewer. Table 2.4 presents the calculations of *deft* for various values of *rho* and average interviews per interviewer. For example, if *rho* is .015 and the average number of interviews per interviewer is about 50, estimates of standard errors should be inflated by a factor of 1.32; that means that an estimate with an intraclass correlation of .015 will have a standard error that is 32 percent larger than an estimate from the same survey that has an intraclass correlation of 0.0.

It is not easy to build a simple mathematical bridge between *defts* and *rhos*, the sampling statistician's measures of interviewer effects, and the psychometrician's measures of reliability and validity. The exact computation depends on the other sources of variance in the survey design. However, validity of a survey measure is (inversely) related to *deft*, as is the standard error of an estimate. The critical point is that from both perspectives, the greater the effect of interviewers on answers and the greater the variance that can be associated with interviewers, the less the value of the data for making precise estimates or valid conclusions about relationships.

We might add an additional important value of standardized interviewing procedures, over and above the significance for interviewer-related error: replicability. It is a tenet of social science that findings should be replicable by other researchers. To the extent that interviewers develop their own ways of asking questions, presenting questions to respondents, and handling respondent problems, the researcher loses the ability to tell other researchers how the data were collected. If a researcher cannot replicate a particular finding, it will be ambiguous whether it was simply an unstable finding in the first place or whether data collection differences affected the results.

The evidence is clear that a lack of standardized interviewing procedures will produce significant, identifiable interviewer-related error. However, only infrequently do researchers design studies so they can estimate the interviewer effects on their data. Even in the absence of measuring interviewer effects, however, maximizing the extent to which interviewers collect data in a consistent, standardized way should be part of good research practice in order to provide the basis for others to replicate research findings.

DETECTING INTERVIEWER-RELATED ERROR

Interviewer-related error is not easy to find. Special measurement efforts are needed to detect it. If one does not make a special effort, it is easy to assume that interviewers have no effect on data. There are three different approaches to identifying interviewer-related error. Each has its own strengths and limitations.

(1) *Direct observation of interviewers*, either by having on-site observers or through tape recordings, is one way of finding out whether interviewers are behaving in ways which we consider to be standardized. From such observations, one can detect whether or not interviewers ask questions as they are written, whether or not their follow-up questions are appropriate, and whether or not they record answers accurately. Many of the findings reported in this book are based on studies of observed or tape recorded interviews (e.g., Hyman, 1954; Cannell, Fowler and Marquis, 1968; Fowler and Mangione, 1986).

Observations of interviewer behavior, however, do not give information about the extent to which interviewers are introducing error into data. Although errors of recording answers can be unambiguously evaluated, the effect of poor question reading or inappropriate probing cannot be directly evaluated. For example, misreading questions often, but by no means always, produces error. Hence, these studies show whether or not interviewers are doing the things we think might influence answers, but do not produce direct evidence of the extent to which they in fact are affecting the data they collect.

(2) *Associating interviewers with the answers* they obtain is a second way to detect interviewer effects. If interviewers are standardized, one should not be able to associate the answers with who did the interview. Some studies have simply addressed the question of whether or not answers could be predicted from the interviewer at all using the intraclass correlation described above (e.g., Kish, 1962; Fowler and Mangione, 1986; Groves and Kahn, 1979; Groves and Magilavy, 1980; Stokes, 1986a; 1986b; Stokes and Yeh, 1988). Other studies have attempted to relate specific interviewer characteristics to the answers obtained (e.g., Schuman and Converse, 1971).

Such studies require special procedures which are not routine in surveys. Specifically, when interviewers are assigned respondents haphazardly or as a matter of convenience, it is not possible to dissociate the effect of interviewers from idiosyncrasies of their samples. In order to do meaningful analysis of interviewer effects on data, one must give each interviewer a representative subsample of the whole sample (or at least a definable part of it). Since that is an unusual design feature, most researchers cannot examine the resulting data to find out whether interviewers are significantly affecting the answers.

(3) *Validating survey answers* when the "true" answer is known from another valid source is a third way to assess error in surveys. Some such studies have compared survey answers with public records, such as voter registration or being convicted of drunken driving (Locander et al., 1976), or against records of health events such as hospitalizations or visits to doctors (e.g., Cannell, Marquis and Laurent, 1977a). Normally, people do surveys because they lack the information they seek to collect. When such validating studies are done, they necessarily have to be restricted to only a few types of information that can be checked, and often the samples are not representative of the general population. Hence, while such studies have proven valuable in adding to our methodological knowledge, they are comparatively rare and they, too, have limits.

The findings reported in this book draw on studies of all of the above types. Although the number of such studies is comparatively small, when they have been done, they have produced ample evidence that interviewers are an important potential source of error in surveys. For example, with respect to studies looking at interviewer procedures, Cannell (1968) found that 35 per cent of the probes used by health interview survey interviewers were classified as directive probes, which are likely to influence answers. Groves and Kahn (1979) published a summary of studies in which interviewer effects had been calculated; they found that on average about one third of the questions used in those studies had interviewer-related intraclass correlations of .015 or higher. As Table 2.3 indicates, if interviewers take an average of 50 interviews each, such an intraclass correlation would in-flate standard errors by 32 percent; obviously the effect on standard errors is greater for questions with higher intraclass correlations.

Looked at from another perspective, Sanders (1962) reported that more than half the variance in the number of health conditions reported in a survey could be attributed to the interviewers.

As an example of results from a study using record checks, Cannell et al. (1977a) found a correlation of .72 between the size of an interviewer's assignment and the percentage of known hospitalizations reported to inter-viewers in a health survey.

CONCLUSION

Using any of the several approaches to detecting interviewer error described above, there is a great deal of evidence that interviewers are an important source of error in surveys. Although it is easy for research organizations and researchers to ignore interviewer-related error, because it is not apparent without special efforts to detect it, there is no doubt that a lack of standardization among interviewers is responsible for a great deal of survey data being less good than it should be. Moreover, in contrast to some strategies for reducing error in surveys, such as increasing sample sizes, the cost of strategies for reducing interviewer-related error are often surprisingly low. On that note, let us turn to what we know about how to minimize interviewer-related error in surveys.

3

Standardized Interviewing Techniques

Although it is not at all easy to carry out a good, standardized survey in which all interviewers behave consistently, the procedures for interviewers to follow in handling the question-and-answer process in a standardized way are simply stated:

1. Read the questions exactly as worded.
2. If the respondent's answer to the initial question is not a complete and adequate answer, probe for clarification and elaboration in a nondirective way; that is, in a way that does not influence the content of the answers that result.
3. Answers should be recorded without interviewer discretion; the answers recorded should reflect what the respondent says, and they should only reflect what the respondent says.
4. The interviewer communicates a neutral, nonjudgemental stance with respect to the substance of answers. The interviewer should not provide any personal information that might imply any particular values or preferences with respect to topics to be covered in the interview, nor should the interviewer provide any feedback to respondents, positive or negative, with respect to the specific content of the answers they provide.

There are, however, two main obstacles to actually carrying out an interview in a standardized way:

1. An inadequate survey instrument. If the questionnaire is not designed so that it can be administered easily in a standardized way, then it is unlikely that standardized procedures will be followed. This is a subject we will say more about in Chapter 5.
2. Respondents do not understand what is expected of them. The measurement process in a survey interview is a team effort, requiring both participants to play their roles as prescribed. A major reason interviewers have difficulty in performing their job properly is that they are unable or do not know how to train the respondent to make the interview process work. That topic is addressed later in this chapter.

There are two other factors that increase the likelihood that interviewers will not do a good job of being standardized interviewers, particularly if they are having trouble with the questionnaire or the respondent:

1. Interviewers generally want answers to be accurate, so they have trouble being standardized when the goals of standardization and accuracy seem to be in conflict.
2. Interviewers like to be personable and responsive to respondents, and they sometimes have trouble being standardized when they feel a conflict between behaving as they are trained and maintaining the kind of relationship they think the respondent wants.

The goal of standardization does not have to conflict with obtaining accurate data or being responsive to the respondent. The last part of this chapter deals with strategies for achieving standardized interviewing without neglecting those other important goals. Table 3.1 provides a summary of the techniques for standardized interviewing and its impediments.

READING QUESTIONS AS WORDED

Virtually every interviewer's manual that we have examined has "reading the questions the way they are written" as a basic first principle of good interviewing technique. On the surface, it would appear to be a rule that is both easy to understand and easy to follow. Hence, it may be somewhat surprising to learn that interviewers often do not read questions the way they are written.

In four studies in which interviewer-respondent interactions were coded, the rates at which interviewers changed question wording ranged from 20 to 40 percent. (Bradburn & Sudman, 1979; Cannell, Fowler & Marquis, 1968; Fowler & Mangione, 1986; Cannell and Oksenberg, 1988.) Moreover, it is important to know that these studies were all done in organizations that put more than the average emphasis on methodological rigor. These numbers are probably conservative with respect to the rates at which interviewers actually change question wording.

Why do interviewers change wording? Certainly in some cases the person who wrote the questions bears major responsibility. Interviewers are likely to change wording if a question is hard to read. They also will change a question to provide an emphasis that they think will make it easier for the respondent to grasp the question or what is wanted. Such explanations, however, can only account for a portion of interviewer lapses. In our opinion, the major force pushing interviewers to change question wording is an effort to make the interaction somewhat more conversational and casual. One way they do that is to add their personal touches to the questions. This practice is likely to continue and grow over an interviewer's career unless

Table 3.1

Standardized Interviewing and Its Impediments

Techniques for Standardized Interviewing
  1. Read questions as written.
  2. Probe inadequate answers nondirectively.
  3. Record answers without discretion.
  4. Be interpersonally nonjudgemental regarding substance of answers.

Obstacles to Standardized Interviewing
  1. Inadequate survey instrument.
  2. Respondents who do not know how to play their role.

Reasons Interviewers Fail to be Standardized
  1. Goal of accuracy seems to conflict with goal of standardization.
  2. Goal of maintaining rapport appears to conflict with goal of standardization.

---

supervisory practices involve monitoring and feedback when interviewers do not read questions exactly as worded. Bradburn and Sudman (1979) found that more experienced interviewers were more casual about the way they read questions than were comparatively new interviewers.

Of course, most of the changes in wording appear to be minor; certainly most interviewers would say they are *basically* reading the questions the way they are written. The critical issue from the point of view of measurement is whether or not the question wording changes that occur make any difference to the quality of measurement. The answer is, we do not know for sure, although we do know that small differences in the way questions are worded can have a major impact on answers.

One way we looked at this was to see whether questions that were most likely to be misread by interviewers were distinctively likely to have large interviewer effects, as measured by the intraclass correlation. Our finding was negative in this respect. When interviewers are given a hard question to read, the changes that they make do not generally produce significant interviewer-related effects on the data.

A second approach was to see whether interviewers who were distinctively casual about question reading seemed to produce distinctively biased data. Our assessment is restricted to 20 interviewers who tape recorded their interviews, which were then coded. Since each interviewer's sample was a probability subsample of the total, it was meaningful to look at whether the estimates derived from an interviewer's subsample differed from the sample as a whole. We simply counted the number of estimates from each interviewer's sample which we thought were potentially biased; that is, that fell in the biased direction compared to the total sample mean. That count was correlated with various ratings of an interviewer's performance with respect to standardized interviewing skills.

It was found that the ratings of various skills, including reading questions, probing, and recording answers, were intercorrelated, so we cannot pull out the distinctive contribution of good question reading from good probing. With only 20 interviewers involved, the raw correlations did not reach statistical significance, but the direction of association for all of these standardized behaviors, including reading questions, is in the expected direction; that is, interviewers who were rated as showing better interviewing skills, including reading questions, appear to obtain less biased data.

The third approach to answering that question is to look at studies of question wording. Schuman and Presser (1981) report a number of experiments in which small changes in question wording were made on purpose, with the results being compared. Basically, they find that sometimes small changes in wording make a big difference in the distribution of answers; in other cases, apparently large changes in question wording have minimal effect on the answers people give.

Question A: Should Communists be forbidden to speak in public places in the United States?

Question B: Should Communists be allowed to speak in public places in the United States?

It could be argued "forbidden" and "not allowed" are equivalent concepts, but to respondents they are not. For example, when comparable samples were asked the two forms of the question, nearly 50 percent said the U.S. should "not allow" Communists to speak in public, while only about 20 percent said the U.S. should "forbid them to speak." This finding suggests that if an interviewer chose to substitute "forbid" for "not allow" in a question, it would have a marked impact on the data, and would produce clear interviewer-related error. Such a change might seem innocuous and conversational to an interviewer, making the question better, if you will, but it would be an excellent example of why we tell interviewers to read questions as worded.

Interviewers also are instructed carefully to read all the alternatives. It might be tempting to add or delete an alternative that says "or do you have no opinion on that topic." Again Schuman and Presser give us a good example that the alternatives matter. Comparable samples were asked whether they favored or opposed a fictitious Agricultural Trade Act of 1978. One sample was explicitly offered the option, "or do you have no opinion on that"; the other sample was offered no such option; it was asked only if it favored or opposed the act. The result: 69% of the sample volunteered that they did not know the answer, but 90% chose the "no opinion" option when it was offered.

Whether or not a "no opinion" category is included has a major effect on the distribution of answers. Not reading one category might seem to be a small change that would make a question easier to read, but it produces interviewer-related error.

On the other hand, Schuman and Presser report other experiments where major changes in wording seem to have little effect on answers. For example, substituting the term "abortion" for the term "end a pregnancy" had no effect on answers that people gave.

In conclusion then, the theoretical argument for having interviewers ask questions exactly the way they are written is easy to understand. If the interviewer does not ask questions the way they are written, the researcher does not know for sure what question was posed. However, general instructions to interviewers not to change wording do not suffice. Interviewers do reword questions unless significant efforts are made to keep them from doing it. Moreover, they are likely to increase the practice over time unless that tendency is checked. The motivations for interviewers rewording questions are generally innocuous, or even constructive, trying to make questions clearer, trying to make the interaction with the respondent go more smoothly, in short trying to improve on the work of the researcher. Sometimes the effects of those efforts are innocuous, but sometimes they create substantial differences. Basically, it takes effort and work on the part of the researcher to write questions that can be asked as worded, but it is an effort that must be made if serious measurement is to be achieved.

PROBING INADEQUATE ANSWERS

In an ideal situation, the researcher writes a great question, the interviewer reads it as written, and the respondent provides a complete answer which meets the question objectives. Of course, that does not always happen. If the initial reading of the question does not produce a satisfactory answer, then the interviewer must engage in some kind of behavior to move the process along and reach the desired end point. The interviewer's behavior cannot be completely preprogrammed, because the problem to be solved will vary from situation to situation. However, the goal is to have interviewers handle the problem in a way that is consistent across interviewers and respondents and that does not influence the content of the answers that result. This behavior, which actually involves several steps, is called non-directive probing.

Actually there are two kinds of problems that interviewers have to solve. First, they sometimes have to clarify the meaning of questions for respondents. Second, they have to stimulate respondents to amplify, clarify, or in some other way modify their original answer to be complete and meet question objectives.

In principle, dealing with the clarification problems should be simple. Most often if a respondent does not understand a question immediately, it merely means the respondent was not attending to some aspect of the question. The interviewer's response is to reread the question in its entirety, emphasizing the words or part of the question that the respondent missed the first time. Although occasionally introductory phrases or sections may be omitted from the second reading, the interviewer should be sure to read the whole question so that the respondent indeed has the same stimulus as all the other respondents when preparing an answer.

In some cases, of course, the problem lies not in the fact that the respondent failed to listen to the question, but that some term or concept in the question had an ambiguous meaning to the respondent. In that case, in our opinion, there is no basis for interviewer discretion. If the term is defined in the question, the interviewer can reread the definition. If the term is not defined in the question, then the respondent must answer the question using whatever interpretation of the term seems best to the respondent.

We know researchers who propose to write definitions of possibly ambiguous terms in training manuals so interviewers can use them when they are asked. We have no hesitation in saying that is a totally inadequate solution to the problem. First, interviewers are not going to open training manuals in the middle of an interview in order to get the exact wording provided by the investigator. Interviewers may attempt to reproduce the definition in the manual from memory, but they will do so inconsistently across respondents and interviewers, producing an unstandardized stimulus. Worst of all, only those respondents who ask or display overt confusion will be exposed to this special definition, while others (including some who are equally confused) will not have the benefit of the definition.

It is absolutely frustrating to respondents and interviewers to have to work with a question where an obviously critical term, that could have more than one meaning, is not well defined. When a respondent asks whether or not visits to psychiatrists count as visits to medical doctors, the response of "whatever you think" may seem to be a ridiculous answer. However, the time to solve the problem is before the data collection begins, not during an interview. The person to solve the problem is the researcher, not the interviewer. Once the data collection has begun, the best measurement will be accomplished if the interviewers consistently present the questions they are given in a standardized way, ill-defined concepts and all.

The other part of the probing task is to obtain answers that meet question objectives. The interviewer activity will depend to some extent on what the task is for the respondent. The respondent task can usefully be categorized into three classes: choosing one of a set of alternative answers provided as part of the question (referred to as a closed-ended question), providing a numerical answer, and providing an answer in the respondent's own words (typically referred to as an open-ended question).

Probing Closed Questions

When a question calls for a respondent to choose an answer from a list, and the respondent has not done so, the interviewer's job is to explain to the respondent that choosing one answer from the list is the way to answer the question (called training the respondent) and to read the list of responses again.

There are two kinds of mistakes that interviewers can make in handling such a situation. First, interviewers can accept an answer that does not exactly fit one of the responses and themselves code the answer into a response category. In short, the interviewer can pick the answer instead of having the respondent do it.

The way this happens is easy to understand.

Interviewer: How would you rate your schools—very good, good, fair, or poor?
Respondent: The schools around here are not very good.

At that point, one can understand why an interviewer might check a box and go on. The problem, of course, is that some interviewers might check the "fair" box and others might check the "poor" box. If the interviewer takes the respondent's words and then does some adjusting to produce an answer, the potential for inconsistency across interviewers is great. When the respondent chooses an answer, it does not guarantee zero error, but it should make the answer dependent only on the respondent and unrelated to the interviewer. This is what standardization is trying to achieve.

The other mistake an interviewer can make in probing a closed-ended question is not to repeat all the alternatives when the alternatives need to be repeated. In the case above, where the respondent said "not very good," it would be understandable if the interviewer probed something like: "Well, would you say fair or poor?" That is bad practice that will affect the answers. It can be shown that the distribution of answers to a scale that has "good, fair, poor" versus one that has "very good, good, fair, poor" is quite different. Respondents respond to the number of categories and the position of a category on a scale, as well as to the words, when classifying themselves. A truncated version of a set of responses is not the same stimulus, and it will affect the answers.

Probing Numerical Answers

When an answer calls for a numerical response, not in categories, the most common problem faced by the interviewer is one of precision. A respondent may answer with a range or a rounded number, and the interviewer may want to attempt to get the respondent to answer more precisely.

One inappropriate behavior is a directive probe. A directive probe is one that increases the likelihood of one answer over others. There are many different ways that interviewers can create directive probes, but the easy way to recognize one is that it can be answered with a "yes" or "no" response. The reason such probes are called directive is that in essence they suggest a particular answer as a possibility. Respondents are more likely to say "yes" than "no" when asked a question like that. So, *any probe that can be answered with a "yes" or "no" is directive*. In addition, any probe that lists or mentions some possible answers, but excludes others, is also directive because it increases the likelihood that the mentioned answers will be chosen.

Questions that call for numerical answers often require interviewers to probe for more specific details, and they are amenable to directive probing.

QUESTION: In the last seven nights, how many times have you gotten fewer than eight hours of sleep?

RESPONSE: I usually get eight hours of sleep.

DIRECTIVE PROBE 1: Well, for the last seven nights, would the answer be 0?

DIRECTIVE PROBE 2: Well, for the last seven nights, would the best answer be 0, 1,or 2?

NONDIRECTIVE PROBE 1: In the last seven nights, how many times have you gotten fewer than eight hours of sleep?

NONDIRECTIVE PROBE 2: Well, for the last week, would the best answer be more than 2 times or 2 or fewer times?

FOLLOW-UP NONDIRECTIVE PROBE 2: (If answer is "fewer") Well, for the past seven days, would the best answer be 0, 1 or 2?

The problem with the first two probes, obviously, is that they suggest an answer. The first is the worst, as it is clearly a probe that can be answered with a "yes" or "no.' The second probe is less blatant, but the interviewer has already pretty well narrowed the field for the respondent. It would take an act of initiative, which respondents often do not do, to give an answer that is different from 0, 1, or 2.

In this case, the very best probe is to repeat the question, since the real problem with the respondent's answer was that the question was not answered. Repeating the question has the distinct advantage of being the most standardized approach also, since it involves no innovation or question creation on the part of the interviewer.

Nondirective Probe #2 is an acceptable response from the point of view of being nondirective, although it is less standardized. In this case, the interviewer is using a technique called "zeroing in." A reasonable guess is made by the interviewer of the general area in which the answer is likely to be found, and then a question is asked which does not suggest an interviewer expectation that the answer will fall on one or the other side of the cutpoint. Once an answer is obtained to the initial question, follow-up questions can be asked to further narrow the range.

Sometimes "zeroing in" is the only way, or the most efficient way, to get respondents to be more precise in their answers. Our own preference, however, is to explain the value of having the respondent, rather than the interviewer or the researcher, make an estimate about where in a range the accurate answer falls, and then to let the respondent, armed with a clarification of his or her role, answer the question as originally posed. In short, as usual, our strategy is to train the respondent and stick with the question as written.

Probing Open-Ended Questions

The hardest probing tasks for interviewers involve those connected with open-ended questions. The interviewer has to make three judgments of any answer that is obtained: Does it answer the question? Is the answer clear? Is the answer complete?

In reviewing manuals for interviewers, we found that there is much greater variation among organizations in their instructions to interviewers about probing than there is about reading questions as worded. Some organizations seem to accept, or even encourage, interviewers to find a variety of conversational ways to get respondents to clarify or elaborate their answers. Our preference is to have interviewers stick with a very small list of probes.

In fact, we train interviewers that in addition to repeating the question, they only need to use three probes:

1. How do you mean that?
2. Tell me more about that.
3. Anything else?

These three probes are easy to remember. They are nondirective. They do not give interviewers any opportunity to innovate in ways that would make their interviews different across respondents or interviewers. Our feeling is that to the extent that organizations encourage innovative probing, any gains that may be realized in variety or conversational interest will be lost in lack of standardization. Moreover, if the creative probes are truly nondirective, they probably amount to one of the three mentioned above.

The interviewer's task is to decide which of those probes is appropriate, and that involves analyzing the respondent's answer. The four probes, including repeating the question, correspond to the four ways in which a respondent's answer can be inadequate:

1. The response can fail to answer the question; it answers some other question. The interviewer should repeat the question.
2. The answer contains unclear concepts or terms that make its meaning ambiguous. The interviewer should probe saying, "How do you mean (that)?"
3. The answer is not detailed enough or specific enough. The interviewer should probe saying, "Could you tell me more about (that)?"
4. A perfectly appropriate answer has been given, but there is a possibility that there are additional points that the respondent could make in answer to the question. The interviewer should ask, "Is there anything else?."

Below are some examples of situations in which these probes would be used.

QUESTION: From your point of view, what are the best things about living in this neighborhood?

COMMENT: This is one of the hardest kinds of questions for interviewers and respondents to deal with, because the kinds of "things" that count are not specified at all. It is up to the respondent and interviewer to decide what sorts of neighborhood features can appropriately be mentioned, and in how much detail.

ANSWER 1: In the last neighborhood in which we lived, it was very transient. People didn't care about keeping up the neighborhood.

COMMENT: The problem with this answer is that it does not answer the question. Although by inference the description of the old neighborhood may be implying something about the characteristics of the present neighborhood, the question asks for a description of the current neighborhood.

PROBE: Repeat the question.

ANSWER 2: The people.

COMMENT: This plausibly could be an answer to this question, but no one could figure out what it means. We need some elaboration.

PROBE: Tell me more about that.

ANSWER 3: The people are good neighbors.

COMMENT: Someone might think that was an adequate answer. It is very hard to tell. One of the problems with this question, as noted, is that it does not give a clue to the interviewer or respondent what kind of answer would satisfy the researcher. Whether or not this is a specific enough answer depends on the question objectives and coding procedures. Nonetheless, what constitutes a "good neighbor" could clearly differ from respondent to respondent, and there is not any information in the answer so far on that topic. A good interviewer would probably probe to find out more about what the respondent meant.

PROBE: How do you mean good neighbor?

ANSWER 4: They keep to themselves. They leave you alone. You don't have to worry about being sociable and you don't have to worry about what they think.

COMMENT: This surprise answer shows the value of probing. Based on the initial answer, some might have expected the "good neighbor" answer was going to lead to a description of how warm, friendly, and helpful everyone in the neighborhood was. We now understand what the respondent means by people and good neighbors. The question, however, calls potentially for the respondent to mention more than one "thing" about the neighborhood.

PROBE: Okay, I have that down. Anything else?

COMMENT: With a question that allows the respondent to make an unlimited number of points, an interviewer should continue to ask "Anything else?," until the respondent says "no."

Probing Don't Know Answers

When the respondent answers a question by saying "I don't know," it poses a special probing problem to interviewers. "I don't know" can be a legitimate answer to a knowledge question. It also can mean:

A. It is a respondent response style, a kind of preface to the answer while he or she is thinking about it.

B. The respondent has not thought about the question before, but if he or she thinks about it, an answer may be forthcoming.

C. The respondent knows an answer, but is not sure it is specific or accurate enough for the standards of the researcher.

When a respondent says "don't know," the interviewer's first task is to attempt to diagnose the origin of the problem.

A. If "I don't know" is considered to be an accurate, thoughtful answer to an information question, the interviewer writes down the answer and goes to the next question.

B. If it is a delaying response style, the interviewer gives the respondent time to think about the answer. The interviewer may want to repeat the question to help the respondent think it through.

C. If the respondent has not thought about the question, the interviewer would encourage the respondent to think about the question, emphasizing that the respondent is uniquely qualified to provide information on the topic. Then repeat the question.

D. If the respondent is not sure about the quality or precision of the answer, the interviewer should be reassuring. There are no right or wrong answers; the questions are designed to get people's own perceptions and opinions. The respondent's own best estimate will be better than not having any information at all. Then the interviewer would repeat the question.

Types of Probing Errors

Probing is certainly the hardest of the interviewer skills to learn. Interviewers make two main types of probing errors: probing directively and failing to probe an answer that requires probing.

Initially, researchers were concerned that interviewers would probe directively in order to make results come out the way they wanted them to be. So, for example, they thought that Republican interviewers would probe in ways that would increase the number of answers supporting Republican views. When interviewers are reasonably well trained, that sort of thing does not seem to happen (e.g., Hyman et al., 1954). Mainly, interviewers seem to probe directively when they think they know the answer the respondent wants to give and are having trouble getting the respondent to be explicit.

Directive probing is a strategy for easing the interviewer-respondent interaction. Interviewers find it stressful when they probe an answer several times and still cannot get the respondent to give an answer that meets the question objectives. When the respondent has said enough that both the interviewer and the respondent are fairly sure that the interviewer knows the answer, the easiest thing for the interviewer to do is to say, "I think you want to answer X; is that right?"

The other kind of error interviewers make is *failure to probe* answers that need to be probed or being inconsistent in choosing which answers they do and do not probe. Three kinds of situations have been found to be particularly prone to interviewer variation in probing.

First, Hyman et al. (1954) found that interviewer expectations affected their probing behavior. Specifically, when they obtained an answer that was consistent with what they expected, based on what they knew about the respondent and other answers given, interviewers tended to accept it without further probing. However, when respondents gave an answer that appeared to interviewers to be inconsistent, they were likely to probe it to make sure they had it right. This is an example of conscientious interviewer behavior that results in handling answers inconsistently.

Interviewers also are likely to be different in the number of answers that they get to questions for which multiple answers are possible. There is interviewer discretion in how often they ask for ''anything else?'' Some interviewers obtain more answers than others on a consistent basis because they consistently probe for more answers, and that affects the data.

Third, interviewers have been found consistently to differ in the way they handle the ''don't know'' response or its equivalent. Some interviewers either work harder or are more successful in getting opinions or answers out of respondents when they say initially that they do not have an answer to the question.

Probing is one part of the question-and-answer process that cannot be completely standardized; if a respondent does not give an adequate answer when the question is first asked, the interviewer has some decisions to make. The response cannot be perfectly programmed. Anytime there is an opportunity for interviewer discretion, there is an opportunity for interviewers to be inconsistent across respondents and across interviewers, and that is when interviewer-related error occurs.

Is probing an important source of error in survey measurement? Absolutely. In Hyman's early studies, differences in probing were the main error-producing aspects of interviewer behavior. The two problems cited above, the way ''don't know'' answers are handled and the number of mentions obtained from respondents, are both characteristics of questions that have been consistently associated with interviewer effects (Groves and Magilavy, 1980). In our own studies, the quality of open-ended probing was related to the bias in answers interviewers obtained at a nearly significant level ($p = .07$). Moreover, as will be discussed in more detail in Chapter 5, the most important correlate of questions which are prone to interviewer effects is the likelihood that they will require interviewer probing.

As we will argue in Chapter 5, we think the most effective way to try to minimize probing as a factor in interviewer-related error is to improve the quality of questions. The less interviewers have to probe, the less opportunity they will have to make errors. In addition, we are strong believers in minimizing the variety of probes that interviewers use. The more interviewers use innovation in creating the stimuli to which respondents respond, the more likely they are to be inconsistent and create error. Moreover, interviewers have plenty to do during an interview besides thinking up innovative probes. A good question will not only minimize the need for probing but will also reduce the inconsistency of probes when they are needed.

RECORDING ANSWERS

The job of the interviewer is to write down the answer the respondent gives. The key to standardized recording is to have no interviewer judgment, no interviewer summaries, no interviewer effects on what is written down. The rules for standardized recording differ for closed and open-ended questions, and by whether the question asks for the report of factual information or information about opinions and feelings. (See Table 3.2.)

For closed-response questions, the key interviewer task is to get the respondent to choose one answer and then to check or record the answer chosen. The only possible recording error, other than a clerical error, would be for an interviewer to indicate that a response was chosen by the respondent when in fact it was not.

The rule for recording open-ended responses to opinion or attitude questions is equally clear and simple: interviewers should write down the answer verbatim; that is, the interviewer should write down the exact words given by the respondent, without summary or omissions. It has been documented that summaries and paraphrases will vary from interviewer to interviewer (e.g., Hyman et al., 1954). One way to keep interviewers from affecting answers is to reduce interviewer discretion about what to record.

When questions are of a factual nature, whether answers are of the closed-response or open-ended variety, the rules are a little bit different. While the coding of subjective answers is highly dependent on the way things are phrased and the particular points that are or are not made, factual questions generally ask for some specific kind of information. The words that a respondent uses are not deemed critical. The interviewer is expected to write down the information provided by the respondent that was called for in the question, without trying to record the exact words. Moreover, if the question includes a set of response alternatives, and the respondent does

Table 3.2
Guidelines for Recording Answers for Different Types of Questions

---

Open-ended, factual questions
  Write down all information relevant to the question's objectives.

Open-ended, opinion questions
  Write down the answer verbatim; use no paraphrasing or summaries.

Closed-ended, factual questions
  Check-off the answer chosen by the respondent.

  If the respondent is not certain which category fits, treat the question as an open question and record all relevant information. The final decision about how to treat the answer should be made during the coding operation.

Closed-ended, opinion questions
  Check-off the answer chosen by the respondent.

  Probe until the respondent chooses an answer.

  Do not check-off an answer category unless the respondent chooses it.

---

not choose one, the best step probably is for the interviewer to write down the relevant information provided by the respondent without necessarily getting the respondent to choose a single category.

One of the important realities about asking factual questions is that sometimes it is hard to anticipate all the possible special circumstances that will be encountered. Moreover, respondents may come up with questions or problems with definitions that are not given in the question but nonetheless are essential to giving an accurate answer. It is not good practice for an interviewer to provide a definition or to give help to one respondent that is not going to be given consistently to others. It is intolerable for an interviewer to make up an idiosyncratic rule about how to handle a special situation that was not anticipated. For a factual question, good practice is to gather all the information needed to answer the question given alternative interpretations of key concepts that effect the answer. Then the researcher can make a consistent coding rule across all respondents.

In an earlier example, we discussed a question about visits to medical doctors. One respondent wanted to know whether a visit to a doctor's office counted when only a nurse was seen for inoculations. If the respondent or interviewer cannot tell from the question what the rule must be, the ideal solution would be to write down all the information needed given either interpretation. Hence, the interviewer might write down: "Four contacts with medical doctor plus a series of ten visits when inoculations were given by a nurse only.''

Another common recording challenge is exemplified by questions about how much formal education has been completed. Many educative post-high school experiences do not fall neatly on the typical educational ladder. Suppose the following categories are offered: less than high school graduate, high school graduate, some college, and college graduate. Respondents will report post-high school education in art, music, nursing, auto mechanics, and many other things. It is not feasible to give interviewers (and thereby respondents) rules for which of these do and do not count as college experience. The thing to do is have interviewers write down the exact pattern of education that the respondent has had, then let the coding department handle these problems consistently across all interviewers and respondents.

So for factual questions, the threat to standardized measurement is that interviewers will make arbitrary decisions. Verbatim recording is not that important, but getting all the information down so that the decision rules can be carefully evaluated and applied consistently is the critical step in standardized measurement for such questions.

Our studies of interviewers suggest that they make relatively few errors in recording closed-response answers. The quality of verbatim recording of open-ended opinion questions varies more. It takes interviewer effort to do that well, and interviewers will not do it unless their supervisors insist on it. It is important, though, because interviewer summaries and paraphrases are not standardized. As noted, Hyman et al. (1954) found that interviewer expectations affected what they wrote down. Interviewers tended to make their recorded answers consistent with their perceptions of the respondent; their paraphrases and summaries left out the contradictions and subtleties in answers.

BEING INTERPERSONALLY NEUTRAL

All interviewer manuals encourage interviewers to be interpersonally neutral as part of the standardization process. Sometimes it is difficult to figure out exactly what is meant by that, but we think the proposed behavior includes, if it is not limited to, the following:

1. The interviewer would not volunteer personal information to the respondent about life situations, views, or values. That would be particularly true for any characteristics that might be related to the subject matter of the interview, but most survey organizations want to minimize such conversation

altogether for at least three reasons. First, volunteering personal information may undermine the goal of establishing a professional, rather than a personal, relationship in which data gathering is the priority. Second, although interviewers cannot be identical in their observable demographic characteristics, talking about personal situations and views only exacerbates the differences across interviewers. Third, information about personal views and background may directly affect answers. The most serious way would be that a respondent would try to guess which answers would be most valued or preferred by interviewers.

2. During the interview interaction, the interviewer should be careful that the feedback provided to respondents does not imply any evaluation or judgment about the content of the respondent's answers. The goal of the interviewer is to get accurate and complete answers. It is natural for respondents to be concerned about how answers will look to the interviewer. The interviewer should be careful not to feed into that process by casual interpersonal behavior.

This aspect of standardized interviewing is something at which interviewers are pretty good if they have at least a little bit of training. Untrained interviewers are not good at it. In our studies, over a third of interviewers with minimal training were rated in need of improvement in the interpersonal area, but over 85 percent of interviews done by interviewers with more than minimal training were judged to be "satisfactory" or better in managing the interpersonal side of things. (See Chapter 7).

These data are consistent with Hyman's studies. He was concerned that interviewers' personal views would be communicated to respondents. He found that respondents usually reported they had no idea about interviewers' opinions. When they did think they knew where interviewers stood, those opinions often were not accurate. Significantly, when respondents thought they knew the interviewer's opinion, they almost always thought interviewers agreed with their views regardless of the interviewer's actual opinions.

In our observations of interview interactions, blatant evaluative comments are quite rare. In training, we tell stories about the interviewer who asked the respondent how much he drinks. When he says he has six drinks a day, the interviewer responds, "Oh my gosh, that's awful." Such events really do not happen in a reasonably well run survey.

What is harder to deal with are the subtle kinds of feedback processes. For instance, a respondent says, "I haven't had to go to the doctor in over a year now. I guess I have been pretty lucky." To that an interviewer might respond, "Isn't that great."

Now what's so bad about that? Don't we all share a general humanitarian wish for universal good health? Sure. However, we do not want that respondent to get the idea that this interviewer will think less of him/her or be unhappy or somehow care if, when the next question comes along, some deviation from perfect health has to be reported. In this instant relationship in which respondents are looking for clues about how to do it right, subtle, seemingly innocent expressions of pleasure that a respondent is healthy or has taken good care of his/her health can lead to effects on the data.

How important is it? It is hard to say for sure. However, Marquis, Cannell and Laurent (1972) found clear evidence that subtle reinforcement of respondent behavior had a significant effect on the number of health conditions and visits to doctors reported. Moreover, in our studies, among tape recorded interviewers, there was a significant relationship between the rating of inappropriate feedback to respondents and the likelihood that interviewers obtained answers that appeared to be biased.

Thus, the evidence is that interviewers can be successful at avoiding blatantly biasing evaluative behavior; most reasonably well run surveys will not have that problem. On the other hand, there is a considerable amount of more subtle interaction that goes on between interviewers and respondents that probably affects some answers.

TRAINING THE RESPONDENT

In our studies, we have come to believe that one of the most important things an interviewer can do to carry out a standardized interview is to train the respondent. Although a main source of problems for interviewers can be a poorly constructed survey instrument, the real problem comes when the interviewer begins to feel awkward because of the way the interview is proceeding and the rules under which the participants are operating. One reaction of interviewers is to bend the rules of standardization in order to appear to be responsive to the respondent and to make the respondent more comfortable. We say a better solution is to explain what is going on to the respondent, the reasons why it is necessary to do the interview in a standardized rather than a nonstandardized way. We are convinced that if interviewers will do this consistently, the quality of the measurement will improve markedly.

There are two basic approaches to training respondents. One is to provide an introductory briefing at the beginning of the interview. The second is to explain specific features of a standardized interview as the issues arise during the course of the interview. Practically speaking, a combination is probably best.

We strongly advocate having interviewers read a paragraph such as the following before the interview starts:

Since many people have never been in an interview exactly like this, let me read you a paragraph that tells a little bit about how it works. I am going to read you a set of questions exactly as they are worded so that every respondent in the survey is answering the same questions. You'll be asked to answer two kinds of questions. In some cases, you'll be asked to answer in your own words. For those questions, I will have to write down your answers word for word. In other cases, you will be given a list of answers and asked to choose the one that fits best. If at any time during the interview you are not clear about what is wanted, be sure to ask me.

This brief introduction accomplishes several very important things that make the job easier for the interviewer. First, it introduces the fact that this is a specialized interaction with a special set of rules. It is not like most other interactions the respondent has been in, including other interviews. It also legitimizes the notion that the interviewer may elaborate or explain further rules as this game progresses.

Second, it tells the respondent in advance what the interviewer is going to do, which will make it easier to do it. Also, once an interviewer has told a respondent that questions will be read exactly as worded, it will make it harder for the interviewer not to do it; it may increase standardization for that reason as well.

Once the interview begins, we believe an interviewer should stop the question-and-answer process every time the respondent fails to perform his or her role appropriately and explain the rules and why the rules matter. The following are among the most common issues:

PROBLEM: The respondent has partially answered, or even fully answered, a question that has not yet been asked. The interviewer feels awkward about reading the next question, since it will appear that the respondent's earlier answer was not heard.

INTERVIEWER: "The next question is one you have already dealt with to some extent. However, the way the interview works is that I need to have you answer each question specifically, so that we can compare the answers you give with the answers everyone else gives. Also, sometimes we find the answer is different to a specific question, even though it seems that the question has been answered before. So, let me read the question as it is worded here, and I would like you to give me the answer to make sure we have it right."

PROBLEM: A question contains a term that the respondent finds ambiguous or not well defined, and the question wording does not provide what the respondent considers to be an adequate definition.

INTERVIEWER: "I see what your problem is with the question. Even though these questions are carefully tested, sometimes we have one that is not quite clear to some people, or which doesn't quite fit everybody's situation. Again, though, the way a survey works, we need people's best answers to the questions as they are written. That way we can compare your answers with other people's. If we change the question for each respondent, we wouldn't be able to analyze the answers. Let me read the question again, and you give me the best, most accurate answer you can, given the way it is written.''

PROBLEM: Respondent does not want to choose one of the response alternatives in a closed-ended question.

INTERVIEWER: "With this kind of question, answers are analyzed according to which of these alternatives people choose. I need to have you choose one of these specific answers so that we can compare your response with those that others give. We know that in some cases none of the answers will fit the way you feel exactly; but other people will have that problem, too. The important thing is that we keep the question-and-answer process consistent across everybody, so we can see similarities and differences in the answers people give.''

PROBLEM: Respondent will not give an answer that is specific enough, because it would only be an estimate or a guess.

INTERVIEWER: "Well we would like it if you would make your very best estimate. Even though it may not be exactly right, no one is in a better position than you are to make this estimate. Just do the best you can.''

PROBLEM: Respondent is speaking too fast, and the interviewer is having trouble recording verbatim.

INTERVIEWER: "I have to write down your answer exactly as you give it, so that it is accurate. If I summarize, I might not get it right. For questions like this, it would help if you would speak slowly, and I may ask you to repeat some parts so that I can get it all down without making a mistake or leaving anything out.

PROBLEM: A family member wants to help a respondent form the answer to an opinion question.

INTERVIEWER: "On factual questions, things like how many times you've seen a doctor or been in the hospital, it is fine for you to get help from anyone who can be helpful, because we want the most accurate information we can get. However, when we ask for somebody's feelings or opinions, there really is no one except you who can give us that answer. Again, it is a matter of being consistent across everybody. When we are asking how somebody feels or what they think, that person alone has to give us the answer that seems to fit best. Although lots of us know others very well, we don't think that anyone else can accurately tell us what someone thinks or feels. Therefore, to be consistent, we make sure that people answer those kinds of questions for themselves.

PROBLEM: The respondent asks the interviewer for an opinion during the interview.

INTERVIEWER: "I'll talk about anything you want after the interview, but not before it is over. The reason is that we have found that in some cases when interviewers give their opinions and ideas during an interview, we influence the answers we get. This whole interview process is set up so that the only thing that influences the answers is your situation and what you have to say."

We could extend this list. The details are not important. What is important is the process. If an interviewer is trying to conduct a standardized interview and the respondent does not know how to play the role, the result will be an awkward interaction in which the interviewer will frequently be forced to choose between standardization and being responsive to the respondent. It is true that in order to train the respondent effectively, the interviewer has to be well informed; the interviewer has to know the rules and have a reasonable idea of the reasons for them. However, that level of knowledge is not difficult to achieve. Most interviewers receive these explanations in the course of their training. The trick is to make sure they use them in the right way during the interview process.

CONCLUSION

Carrying out an interview in a standardized way is a difficult task. From the point of view of skills, there is no doubt that probing is the hardest thing for interviewers to do in a consistent, nondirective way. It is the area in which interviewers are most likely to fall short of reasonable standards, and also the area from which interviewer effects are most likely to emanate. Recording open-ended answers to opinion questions is also very hard to do well, and also is a source of error, though the decline of the use of open-ended questions in standardized surveys makes that somewhat less of a problem than in the past.

Interviewers also do not read questions as worded; they like to make changes in questions. As a source of error in surveys, reading errors probably are less important than probing errors. However, the rates at which interviewers have been found to be writing their own questions in published studies does not make one sanguine about that aspect of standardization. Moreover, it is likely that in more casually operated surveys, the rates at which interviewers are changing question wording are even more severe, with more severe consequences, than those reported in the literature. Although it is hard to document the exact extent of that, it may be worth repeating that the bedrock of standardized measurement is that we know what questions people are being asked.

Being neutral is something that interviewers seem to understand and take to readily. Again, the perspective in this book may be slanted by the fact that people who study interviewers tend to work with well organized interviewing staffs where clear standards are emphasized. The ease with which interviewers can slip into interpersonal behavior that implies judgment and evaluation leads one to suspect that this, too, may be more of a problem than is reflected in published data.

Finally, one of the most important contributions we have to make to improving the standardization of interviewing is to emphasize the importance of training the respondent. Based on our observations, a main reason for a breakdown in standardization is that respondents fail to cooperate or fail to understand the process. Consider the task of trying to play chess with someone who thought he or she was playing a slight variation on checkers. There would be a general idea about what was supposed to happen, but confusion about the detailed rules would make it an extremely frustrating experience. In a way, survey respondents are in a similar situation. They have a general idea about interviews, but they do not have a clear understanding about how a specific standardized interview should work. Telling them that the rules are different, and then briefing them on the details of the rules as they become relevant in the course of the game, only makes sense, and it makes for a much better game.

4

Establishing the Context for Standardized Interviews

A precondition to successfully carry out a standardized interview is to establish relationships in which the respondents are willing, and the interviewers able, to carry out their respective roles in the measurement process.

Most thinking and writing about interviewing has focused on the quality of the question–and–answer process and how that is managed. Additionally, the important contribution of Charles Cannell and his associates has been to focus attention on the importance of the context in which that question–and–answer process occurs and to point to the critical role that interviewers play in setting up the interview as a measurement experience. There is no doubt that the way the question-and-answer process is handled plays an important role in the quality of measurement, as discussed in Chapter 3. However, there also is no doubt that the way the interviewer sets up the interview interaction, the relationship with the respondent within which the question- and-answer process occurs, also plays a critical role in the quality of the data that result. Moreover, that responsibility rests heavily with the interviewer. It is a very demanding part of the interviewer's job, and it is one that has been found to be done inconsistently by interviewers.

In this chapter we discuss three important aspects of setting up the interviewer-respondent interaction.

1. Explaining the purpose or reason for the interview. Respondents must have some reason for contributing their time for an interview, and there must be some sense of what will be accomplished by so doing. In the first section of this chapter, we discuss what is known about why respondents give interviews and what difference their motivations make for the quality of data that result.

2. Establishing the tone of the relationship between the interviewer and respondent. On the one hand, the relationship needs to be positive enough so that the respondent wants to give the interview and be cooperative. On the other hand, it also has to be the kind of relationship in which answering the questions accurately and completely is seen as appropriate and desirable. In the second part of the chapter we will discuss what we know about how to formulate that relationship and how that affects the quality of measurement.

3. Communicating the goals of the interview and the standards that will be applied. Specifically, the interviewer is in charge and sets the standards for how hard the respondent is supposed to work and how seriously the task is to be taken. This aspect of the interaction has proven to be one of the most important in affecting the quality of measurement that results. That will be the focus of the last section of this chapter.

RESPONDENT REASONS FOR PARTICIPATING IN SURVEYS

Most survey interviews take place in the context of an "instant relationship"; that is, in a very short period of time with very little background or history, the interviewer introduces the task, explains its purposes, establishes some sort of relationship with the respondent, and communicates to the respondent what he or she is supposed to do.

Prior to initial contact from an interviewer, either by a personal visit to the respondent's home or a telephone call, the respondent may have received an advance letter describing the purposes and sponsorship of the research project. In recent years, an increasing number of interviews, probably the majority, are done by telephone using random-digit dialing techniques. With such procedures, there is no possibility of any advance notice; the researcher does not even know whether or not a residential household will be attached to the telephone number that is dialed until someone answers the phone and answers a few questions.

Consider the following scenario:

INTERVIEWER: Hello, have I reached (617) 956-1150?

RESPONDENT: Yes you have.

INTERVIEWER: Is this a residential or business telephone?

RESPONDENT: Residential I guess. Why do you want to know?

INTERVIEWER: Well, my name is Mary Smith. I work for the Survey Research Center at the State University. We are doing a study of people's concerns about AIDS, funded by the federal government. We are interviewing a sample of adults throughout the state. In order to know which person in your household I am to interview, I need to know how many adults are living there in the household with you aged 18 or older? (NOTE: Because many surveys require interviewers to follow guidelines for choosing whom to interview in a household, it is common for the first question or two to be about who lives in the household).

RESPONDENT: Well, I live here by myself.
INTERVIEWER: Well then, you are the person I want to interview. If this is a good time, why don't we do the interview right now?

After an interaction that goes very much like the above, the interviewer will give some further description of the project and the respondent's task, then proceed to ask the respondent a series of questions.

It hardly need be said that what a respondent is going to be asked to do after an interaction like that, and for what purpose, varies widely. Surveys are sponsored by manufacturers and sellers of commercial products, by political candidates, by newspapers, by state and federal governments, and by foundations. There is hardly any topic that has not been covered in a survey. The questions the respondent may be asked to deal with could range anywhere from the brand of toothpaste the respondent uses or the respondent's voting preferences to whether or not the respondent engages in activities that relate to increased risk of AIDS. The length of the interview may be a few minutes to over two hours.

Demands on respondents can vary in other ways. Some questions ask for information about impressions or feelings that require little thought. Other surveys ask for detailed information about health expenditures over the year for the entire family, which may require respondents to consult records and other household members in order to provide accurate data. Respondents may be asked to choose responses from a short list of alternatives, or they may be asked to answer questions in their own words, and elaborate at length on their thoughts. The contribution of this effort to the world can range from helping a manufacturer sell more toothpaste to helping a candidate get elected to providing basic information needed to set health insurance policy or to estimate the cost of a health insurance program. No matter what the respondent is asked to do or why, the researcher hopes that the interview process will produce good measurement and that the answers will provide precise and valid descriptions of the populations studied.

One way of looking at the demand on respondents is the amount of time or effort that will be needed for the interview. Another aspect of the demand is whether the respondent will be asked to provide any information that might be considered personal or might potentially entail some risk, such as reporting drug use or embarrassing personal behaviors. Whether or not the respondent performs the required task well must, at some level, depend on the respondent's motivations for participating and how the interview situation is perceived.

Respondent Typologies à la Kelman

One way of thinking about the orientation of a respondent to the interview that has proved helpful to us builds on work by Kelman (1953), who studied influence relationships. Obviously, the interviewer-respondent interaction is an example of an influence situation, where the interviewer is trying to set up a relationship in which the respondent will cooperate and perform a task in a way the interviewer specifies.

Kelman identified three kinds of influence relationships that differed in their dynamics.

Compliance characterizes those relationships where influence is managed by manipulating punishments and rewards contingent upon behavior. A respondent who cannot say "no," who cannot find a good reason to get rid of the interviewer, and hence gives the interview simply to avoid an unpleasant interaction might be a good example of a compliant respondent. A respondent whose primary orientation was to have a positive interaction with the interviewer, who wanted praise or the pleasure of interaction, is also an example of a compliant respondent. The critical problem with inducing respondents to participate in the interview via compliance is that the quality of their role performance that matters most, the accuracy of reporting, cannot be easily detected. A respondent can appear to be performing the role well without doing a good job at all. Hence, rewards are unlikely consistently to produce the kind of behavior the researcher most wants to encourage.

Identification is the name Kelman gives to a second kind of influence. This kind of influence stems from a person's accepting a role in a relationship, and then behaving in a way that is consistent with the role expectations. In the case of being a respondent, there are several roles that might be activated. The role of being a good citizen who is helpful to good causes is potentially the most salient role to social science surveys. A more limited role, which may work just as well, is being a nice person who is cooperative and tries to be helpful to others when presented with a legitimate request. The effectiveness of this kind of relationship to generate good reporting in an interview depends most of all on the respondent's perceptions of what the role entails.

Internalization is Kelman's term for a third kind of influence relationship. Influence can occur because links are forged between certain behaviors and a person's own values. In the case of an interview, a respondent would see participating in the interview as a way of achieving personal goals such as providing social service or learning more about an important social problem. Once again, as with identification, the success of the influence strategy in producing good reporting will depend on the respondent's seeing that giving complete and accurate answers is the best way to achieve his or her goals.

Respondent Orientation to Interviews

To evaluate whether Kelman's typology is useful when thinking about an interview, we should know something about the orientation of respondents to the interview. There are two studies on which we have to draw for information about this topic. In both cases, respondents were reinterviewed a day or two after they participated in a 30-minute health interview about how they felt about the original health interview experience. The procedures for the two original health interviews were fairly similar. Both health studies sent an advance letter to respondents explaining the purpose of the study, followed shortly thereafter by a visit from an interviewer to respondents' homes. The auspices of the two studies and their general purposes differed considerably. A University of Michigan study, done in the 1960's, focused on the National Health Interview Survey (Cannell, Fowler & Marquis, 1965b). That survey was carried out by the Bureau of the Census interviewers under contract to the Public Health Service to collect national data. The study in the Boston area (Fowler and Mangione, 1986) featured interviewers employed by the Center for Survey Research, University of Massachusetts, working under a grant from the Federal government to collect data for local health planning purposes. The questions that respondents were asked varied considerably between the two studies, but taken together, the two studies provide a fairly consistent picture.

PRINCIPLE 1: Respondents vary greatly in the amount of information they have about a survey and many people participate in surveys with little or no information about its sponsorship or purposes. The most striking demonstration of that was found in the Michigan study of the Health Interview Survey. As noted above, respondents received an advance letter, a standard introduction by the interviewer, and they were left with a thank-you note that described the sponsorship. Nonetheless, when interviewed the next day about the survey, nearly half said they did not know what the purposes of the study were and nearly half said they did not know for whom the interviewer worked. Indeed, even though the Bureau of the Census is probably the most visible survey organization in the country, only about one in ten respondents was able to correctly identify the Bureau of the Census (see Table 4.1).

The answers were highly related to the education level of the respondent. Since the education level in the country as a whole has shifted up-

ward since the 1960's when that study was done, the average proportion
of respondents who are informed may be higher now than in that study.
Of people who had been to college, two-thirds had a reasonably clear idea
about the purposes of the study and 60% identified either the Bureau of
the Census or a federal health agency as the employer of the interviewer.
Nonetheless, given the fact that the majority of survey research is done with
less attention to introducing the study and less readily identifiable spon-
sors, it seems almost certain that in normal survey practice many respondents
are not going to be highly informed.

*PRINCIPLE 2: Interviews are not a very important event in most
respondents' lives.* Again, the support for this principle comes from the
Michigan study of the Health Interview Survey. Reinterviewed respondents
were asked whether they had thought about the interview at all after it was
over, and whether they had talked with friends or relatives about the interview after it was over. About 40% of the people said they had not thought
about the interview after the interviewer had left; a similar overlapping 40%
said they had not talked with anyone about the interview after the interviewer had left.

In a somewhat more direct approach to measuring importance,
respondents in the Boston area survey were asked how important they considered the research in which they had participated. While 44% said they
considered it "very important," 47% thought that "fairly important"
described their feelings best, and 9% thought that "not important" was
the best description.

Consistent with the variety and range of information that respondents
have about surveys, they also report participating in surveys for different
reasons. Again the most direct information on this topic comes from the
Michigan study of the Health Interview Survey. Respondents were asked
to look at a picture of a respondent with an interviewer at the door and
to report what kinds of positive and negative feelings they thought it likely
the respondent was having at that time (Table 4.2).

The two most salient reasons for producing a positive reaction were the
interest in being of service and the chance to interact with the interviewer.
On the negative side, the most common reason expressed for negative reactions to the interview (if one puts together the two middle categories in Table
4.2) is the respondent's inability to link his or her goals to participation
in the survey. Being busy or having other time demands when the interviewer called is the next most common response. Concern about the questions, either being personal questions or questions that are difficult to answer,
was consistently the least mentioned problem with the interview experience,
though that might be different for interview topics other than health.

Table 4.1

Measures of Respondent Information About the Health Interview Survey
by Respondent Education

	0-8 Years Grade School	1-3 Years High School	4 Years High School	1 or More Years College
Rating of information about purposes of study				
Clear	27%	45%	41%	67%
Vague	14	13	15	7
Don't Know	59	42	44	26
	100%	100%	100%	100%
Who employed interviewer				
Bureau of the Census	2%	9%	14%	18%
Federal Health Agency	13	11	22	42
Health Department	15	15	15	13
Government	8	2	12	0
Other	3	3	4	6
Don't Know	59	60	33	21
	100%	100%	100%	100%
N	(129)	(89)	(123)	(67)

SOURCE: Adapted from Fowler (1966).

When one puts these data together, the important conclusion is that people's reasons for participating in surveys and their orientation to surveys are not consistent. Moreover, although we know of no exhaustive attempts to improve the quality of respondent information about what they are doing, we know of two efforts that suggest that such efforts are likely not to be successful.

One example was carried out at the University of Michigan (Cannell, Fowler & Marquis, 1965c). A professional artist was commissioned to design advance materials that would be more engaging and communicate more information to respondents. These materials were then sent to respondents, and they were subsequently interviewed about their reaction to the information they had obtained. Only about half the respondents reported reading it "very well," as compared with just "glancing" at it; nearly a third did not remember receiving it at all. New improved brochures did not have any discernible effect on readership.

Further afield, but potentially relevant, is the literature on informed consent in medicine. This is another situation where people are trying to bring

Table 4.2

Respondent Perceptions of Why People Would React Positively
to an Interview

Positive factors:	Percent of Total Positive Factors Mentioned
Being of help or service	35%
Like talking with interviewer	35
Enjoyed something about the questions	5
Desire for personal benefit	11
Like chance to rest	14
	100%
	N (314)

Respondent Perceptions of Why People Would React Negatively
to an Interview

Negative factors:	Percent of Total Negative Factors Mentioned
Busy—took too much time	37%
Survey not worthwhile	14
Don't know enough about purpose	29
Problem with questionnaire content	20
	100%
	N (796)

SOURCE: Adapted from Cannell et al. (1965b).

a patient up to a reasonable standard of information and understanding in a comparatively short period of time. Post tests of how well informed patients are after going through a standard information-giving experience indicate wide variability in how well the information is absorbed (e.g., Meisel & Roth, 1983).

Although there may be more effective ways to communicate information to respondents, our conclusion is that survey researchers have to assume that there will be considerable variation in how well informed participants are. Moreover, that in itself ensures that there will be variation in the orientation of respondents to the task.

Going back to the models of influence with which we began this discussion, the critical question, of course, is whether or not what the respondent feels, thinks or knows about the interview makes any difference to the quality of data. Although the data are not definitive on that topic, the evidence tends to support the notion that there are not major differences.

In the Michigan study there was an extensive effort to link the positive and negative forces respondents reported to the quality of their reporting (Cannell, Fowler & Marquis, 1968). There was some evidence that interviewing respondents at a time that they found inconvenient, when they said they were busy, such as at mealtime, produced worse reporting. However, there was no evidence that respondents who reported a positive orientation toward interacting with the interviewer were worse or better reporters than those who reported no such interest. There also was no evidence that respondents who cited an interest in being helpful or of being of public service were better respondents than those who did not cite such an interest. There was a slight tendency for the better educated respondents, those who had finished high school, to report more health information when they had a higher level of information about the purposes and sponsorship of the study. That relationship, however, was modest, and there was no such relationship for those who had not finished high school (Fowler, 1966).

Although there is no direct evidence, we still believe compliance is the worst reason for respondents to participate in an interview. Quite simply, it is very difficult for interviewers to link specific rewards or punishments to the *quality* of reporting by a respondent. Having a respondent oriented toward achieving some direct personal goal, such as being paid for the interview or avoiding having to say "no" to an interviewer, rather than providing accurate and complete answers, is likely to be a counterproductive orientation that will lead to distortion as often as it leads to accuracy. However, based on what we know at the moment, we see no reason to think that whether a respondent is motivated in an interview by desire to actualize his or her own values (internalization) or to play out a relationship with the interviewer (identification) makes any difference to the quality of data that will result. From our perspective, the critical aspect of either of those orientations is the extent to which it is clear to respondents that good reporting is the way to play out their respondent role. How we achieve that is the topic of the last part of this chapter.

THE INTERVIEWER-RESPONDENT RELATIONSHIP

The above discussion emphasizes the importance of the relationship between interviewer and respondent for some respondents. Given the uneven level of information that most respondents have about the background and purposes of surveys, the reaction to the interviewer is probably critical for the majority of respondents in granting an interview. Moreover, that relationship with the interviewer will have a major effect on how the respondent performs his part of the measurement process.

We have noted that in most surveys the interviewer-respondent relationship is established in only a few minutes of interaction. Moreover, on the telephone, the respondent lacks even visual cues to go along with auditory cues to help form an impression of the interviewer and define the role. In this situation, it seems almost certain that respondents draw upon other role relationships with which they are familiar to try to define the situation. It may make a great deal of difference which role model is chosen.

One particularly critical issue is that the ideal role relationship between interviewer and respondent has several different, possibly antagonistic dimensions. On the one hand, the interviewer should be someone who can generate some trust and respect. The respondent must be convinced that the interview is being done for a reasonably good cause and that the interviewer's assurances of no risk or harm to the respondent are legitimate. In addition, we want the interviewer to structure the interaction, so it would be good if the interviewer were someone who appeared to comfortably occupy a role of authority and respect. This would suggest that interviewers should be viewed as a teacher, doctor, lawyer, or social worker.

On the other hand, it is not uncommon for interviewers to ask respondents to give information that may seem personal, potentially embarrassing, or even involve some risk or threat. What is the best role model in that situation? One idea is that a good friend is the sort of person to whom one might tell personal information that would be more difficult to tell to a stranger. On the other hand, it may be unrealistic to think that in two minutes an interviewer can assume the role of a confidant. One might consider taking on the role of a neighbor. However, it may be that respondents will be less likely, rather than more likely, to want to divulge personal information to someone they know casually as compared with a complete stranger, who is also seen as a professional.

An additional consideration, however, is that an interview should occur in a context in which communication flows freely. The authority figure models, such as physician or teacher, may create a context in which respondents feel they must produce the right answers, or sophisticated answers, rather than responding openly to the question.

In summary, we want a warm, professional relationship, one in which the interviewer is respected and trusted, but nonetheless the kind of professional who is accepting and nonjudgmental.

With this kind of description, the image of a psychotherapist or counselor comes to mind, and it is not surprising that the terminology and even techniques of therapists, such as Carl Rogers, have come to play an important role in the terminology and functioning of standardized survey interviewing. Still, one can certainly ask how successful most interviewers are in establishing a pseudo-therapeutic relationship with the person who answers the telephone after some random digits have been dialed.

Once again, there are only two studies of which we are aware that produce data about the kinds of relationships interviewers form with respondents which permit any assessment of how that affects the quality of data. Moreover, again, both of these studies dealt with surveys carried out in people's homes. We have to infer how these findings might compare to results for telephone interviewers or for interviewers in other settings.

One answer to the question of what kind of image respondents have of interviewers comes from the Michigan study of the Health Interview Survey. Table 4.3 shows respondent answers about the kinds of people interviewers most and least reminded them of. It will be reassuring to interviewers to learn that predominantly the image they create is of a professional. Social workers, nurses, and teachers were the three most commonly cited answers to the question. However, there was some heterogeneity, and 19% thought the interviewer was most like a neighbor or close friend, about the same number as thought the interviewer was least like a neighbor or close friend. Contrary to some predictions, the image of a door-to-door salesman did not describe the interviewer well at all for most respondents.

If the image of a professional is the most common one aroused by interviewers, there certainly is no agreement about how an interviewer should behave. In fact, respondents to the Michigan survey were equally divided about whether they preferred the interviewer to be primarily "businesslike" or whether they would prefer that the interviewer spend some time "visiting" (Table 4.4). There was a relationship to those answers with education; the less the education the respondent had, the more likely to be interested in having the interviewer "visit."

Despite this apparent diversity in preference in interviewer style, the overwhelming conclusion from respondents reports is that they like their interviewers. For example, 88% of the respondents in the Michigan study said that the interviewer they had should neither have been more businesslike nor more friendly. In the Boston area study, the average rating by respondents of interviewers was nine or above on a scale from one to ten with respect to professionalism and friendliness, as well as several other ratings; over 90% of respondents said the interviewers did an "excellent" (58%) or "very good" (33%) job. Although there obviously is some tendency for respondents to be reluctant to criticize interviewers, the data from both of these studies are overwhelming that respondents react quite favorably to interviewers.

Table 4.3

Distribution of Respondent Reports of What Interviewer Was Most Like,
Next Most Like, and Least Like

Interviewer was:	Most Like	Next Most Like	Least Like
Professionals			
Nurse	7%	13%	3%
Social Worker	46	16	2
Female Doctor	2	5	6
Teacher	3	13	5
Female Lawyer	2	2	21
Clerical and Sales			
Secretary or Clerk in Office	14	15	4
Salesgirl in Store	1	4	12
Door-to-door Salesman	3	6	17
Nonprofessionals			
Neighbor	12	9	6
Community Chest Volunteer	1	6	7
Close Friend	7	7	15
Not ascertained	2	4	2
	100%	100%	100%
N = 412			

SOURCE: Adapted from Cannell et al. (1965b, Table 8.7, p. 77).

If the overall image of interviewers is very favorable from the point of view of respondents, the question still remains as to whether or not there are certain interviewer styles which are more or less conducive to good reporting. The answer to that is "maybe."

In the Michigan study interviewers were found to differ in the extent to which they were at all responsive when respondents initiated conversation that digressed from the interview, in the extent to which they initiated humor, and in the extent to which they seemed to have related personally to the respondents, for example, by staying after the interview and chatting for a minute or two. If those behaviors can be interpreted as indicating a more interpersonal or respondent-oriented approach to the interview, there was some slight evidence that such behaviors were associated with better reporting of health events by respondents who had not finished high school. However, there were no such relationships for respondents who had graduated from high school or gone beyond that in education (Fowler, 1966). In the Boston study, there was some tendency for interviewers who were rated as more friendly by their respondents to obtain answers that were less biased. However, Weiss (1968) in a study that will be discussed more in

Table 4.4

Answers to Question 37: "Some people say they would rather an interviewer be businesslike—stick to her job—while some say they would rather the interviewer visit a little. Which would you like best?"

How should interviewer behave?	
Only businesslike mentioned	36%
Businesslike stressed more	3
Both equally stressed	12
Visit stressed more	5
Only visit mentioned	39
Other	0
Not ascertained	5
	100%
N = 412	

SOURCE: Adapted from Cannell et al. (1965b, Table 8.8, pg. 79).

Chapter 6, reported evidence that when interviewers rate their "rapport" with respondents high, the result tends to more biased data. Hensen (1973) manipulated interviewer style, with interviewers sometimes behaving in a more interpersonal way, other times in a more professional way. The results showed no significant differences in the accuracy of reporting, though there was evidence that the "professional" style produced better data for one subclass of events reported.

Thus, for many respondents, the interviewer is the key reason why they are doing the interview and the key potential motivator for the way they perform their task. However, there is variety in the way that interviewers establish a relationship with respondents, and the evidence is modest that there is one particular style of interacting with respondents which is best.

Observers tend to agree that basically the interaction between the interviewer and the respondent should be a professional one, one which is focussed on the task and in which concerns about interpersonal attractiveness are minimized for respondents. However, it is clear that an interview also must be an interaction in which communication flows freely, and there is some evidence from both the Michigan study and the Boston area study that interviewer efforts, in moderation, to relax the relationship and make it somewhat more interpersonal may be beneficial for some respondents, perhaps most particularly those who have not finished high school. Respondent tastes and interviewer styles clearly differ, and it is almost certain that there is no single best way to build an interviewer-respondent relationship. What is important is the role expectations that are built into that relationship, regardless of its particular tone, and it is that topic to which we turn our attention.

SETTING STANDARDS FOR THE RESPONDENT

There is a great deal of evidence that the standards interviewers communicate to respondents for how they are to perform their jobs has a major impact on the quality of data that comes out of an interview.

In order to understand this section, it is important to appreciate that respondents do not know what is expected of them when they come into an interview situation. Some of the knowledge they lack has to do simply with the specific rules of a survey interview. A standardized interview, as we have described, is special in that interviewers ask questions as worded, give only limited explanations about what is expected beyond the initial question, and write down answers verbatim. It is a measurement process, with very structured procedures, and somehow the respondent must get the idea about how that role is played. The interviewer is the one who has to be the teacher.

In addition, there is the question of the standards for the respondent's performance. Is this a serious measurement process, or are we simply filling out the questionnaire? Are exact answers needed, or will general ideas suffice? Is this basically a polite, friendly conversation, or is this a serious social science investigation for which great accuracy is required?

These are the kinds of issues that have a very important effect on the quality of respondent answers. In Chapter 3, we discussed the importance of the interviewer training the respondent in the detailed rules of the standardized interview. In this chapter, we talk about the way the standards for performance in the interview interaction are set up by the interviewer.

One of the surprises that emerged from Cannell's pioneering observations of interview interactions was how much behavior went on in an interview that was not directly part of the question-and-answer process. About 50% of everything the interviewers said after the interview started was something other than a question or a probe (Cannell et al., 1968). This was not simply chatting, though some "visiting" did occur. These were businesslike interviewers. Mainly the interaction related to the task. Moreover, studies of respondent perceptions and interviewer behaviors suggested some interesting correlates of reporting quality that had not appeared in the literature before.

Respondents were asked about their perceptions of what was wanted in the health interview. They split on one very interesting question: Whether interviewers wanted them to give "exact answers" or whether "general ideas" were good enough. Moreover, whether the respondent thought exact answers or general ideas were required turned out to correlate significantly with the quality of reporting; those who thought interviewers wanted exact answers also seemed to report better (Table 4.5). Fowler (1966) found this to be particularly the case for respondents with a high school education or more. A similar question, asking whether interviewers wanted everything reported or just important things, showed a similar, though less striking pattern.

Another indication of the importance of standards came from interviewer reports about their concerns when they were interviewing. Interviewers who most often expressed a concern about obtaining accurate answers in fact appeared to obtain better reporting (Table 4.5). Again, this pattern was most pronounced for respondents who were at least high school graduates.

Fowler (1966) provided an analysis that pulled these findings together. He found that at least among high school graduates, the concerns interviewers expressed in a general interview about their work showed up in their respondents' perception of whether exact or general answers were required in the health interview. Specifically, interviewers most concerned about accuracy were more likely to have respondents who reported "exact" answers were needed, interviewers who were most concerned about efficiency were less likely than average to think that exact answers were needed (Table 4.6).

These data, while not definitive in themselves, laid the ground work for a series of explorations that turned out to provide some of the best and most important findings generated to date about how to improve the quality of interviewing and improve the quality of survey based estimates.

One early indication of the important role that interviewers had in setting standards for performance emerged from a comparison of interviewer and self-administered questions about hospitalization (Cannell & Fowler, 1964). In this study, a sample of households known to have had at least one person hospitalized during the year was used. The households were randomly assigned to several different treatments. In one group, interviewers carried out a health survey, but did not ask any questions about hospitalization. Rather, when they got to the end of the interview, they gave the respondent a questionnaire to be filled out after the interviewer had left regarding hospitalizations for the family during the preceding year. In other treatments, the interviewer asked all the same health questions and, in addition, asked the hospitalization questions, too.

A distinctive strength of this study was that there was a firm criterion for accuracy, namely the percentage of known hospitalizations that was reported as determined by matching interview reports against hospital records. Moreover, because of the way the sample was assigned to interviewers, it was possible to calculate a meaningful rate for each interviewer

Table 4.5
Summary of Correlates of Reporting Quality
Related to Standards for Performance

| | *Reporting Index** | | | | |
Respondent Reports Interviewer Wanted	*Low*	*Medium*	*High*	*Total*	*N*
Exact answers	30%	38	32	100%	223
General ideas	38%	39	23	100%	168
Everything, no matter how small	32%	40	29	100%	312
Only fairly important things	39%	36	25	100%	80
Interviewer Concern About Accuracy					
High	29%	36	35	100%	140
Medium	39%	39	22	100%	139
Low	33%	34	23	100%	133

SOURCE: Adapted from Cannell et al. (1968).
NOTE: *This is an index of the relative number of conditions reported, adjusted for the age of the respondent.

of the percentage of known hospitalizations which were reported. Each interviewer had samples that were subjected to each treatment, so that some of each interviewer's respondents answered questions asked by the interviewer and others filled out self-administered questionnaires on the same topic. When results were analyzed by interviewer, the surprising finding was that there was a high correlation between how well an interviewer's respondents reported in person and how well they reported in a self administered form. That is, if an interviewer's respondents were likely to report known hospitalizations in person, they were also highly likely to do so in the self-administered form.

The importance of that finding was what it implied about the way that interviewers obtained good reporting. Previously, most of the focus had been on the way that the question-and-answer process was handled. However, obviously the interviewer had nothing to do with the question-and-answer process for the self-administered portion of the study. Rather, it had to be that some interviewers motivated or set standards for their respondents, which carried over to their performance when they filled out self-administered forms. That study was one of the earliest and most cogent demonstrations of the importance of setting standards as a mechanism for affecting the quality of data that results from surveys.

Cannell then began to look in more detail at the kinds of interactions that took place between interviewers and respondents for clues to the way in which interviewers were influencing the quality of answers. One of the clear differences he detected among interviewers was the pace at which they conducted the interview. Some interviewers read very quickly, others speak

Table 4.6

Respondent Perception of Interview Standards by Interviewer Concern
About Efficiency and Accuracy for High School Graduates Only

Interviewer concern about efficiency	Respondent Said Interviewer Wanted			
	Exact answers	General ideas	Total	N
Low	77%	23	100%	62
Medium	62%	38	100%	81
High	66%	34	100%	47
Interviewer concern about accuracy				
Low	62%	38	100%	104
High	76%	24	100%	86

SOURCE: Adapted from Fowler (1966), Tables 7.3 and 7.4, pp. 158-159.

slowly and distinctly. Some give respondents time to consider their answers after they have given them, while others begin asking the next question as soon as one answer has been given. Fowler (1966) found that the pace at which the interviewer conducts the interview is a significant correlate of the respondent's perception of the task. If interviewers go fast, respondents conclude that accurate and complete answers are less important than quick answers. To our knowledge, a direct link between pace and data quality has not been documented. However, we think it is likely that having interviewers speak slowly is one important and practical way in which researchers can increase the standardization across interviews. In addition, Cannell has tested four different strategies that have now been demonstrated as effective ways for interviewers to improve the quality of reporting.

Reinforcement

Cannell and his associates, notably Marquis et al. (1972), found that interviewers differed in the kinds of respondent behaviors that they reinforced. In many cases, interviewers were reinforcing counterproductive behaviors. When some interviewers feel uncomfortable in the interview situation, which is particularly likely with a reluctant respondent who is ambivalent toward the whole interview, their strategy is to try to make the respondent feel better. Inadvertently, the result is that the interviewers say encouraging things ("that's good" or "that's fine") when any answer at all is obtained, even if it is not thoughtful. In fact, even when the respondent refuses to answer a question, interviewers are likely to be encouraging and ingratiating.

Marquis designed an experiment in which interviewers were programmed to reinforce constructive respondent behaviors. Thus, when a respondent gave an answer that seemed to be thoughtful or complete, at some rate the interviewers would say something positive about the respondents' performance (not about specific answers, of course). Interviewers were also trained not to give positive feedback when respondents gave a quick answer or said "no" in a way that appeared not to be thoughtful. Although the effects were somewhat inconsistent (and seemed to affect less educated respondents most) there was clear evidence of an increase in the number of health conditions reported under the patterned reinforcement procedure compared with the procedure where interviewers reinforced behavior on their own. This result was replicated by Cannell, Oksenberg and Converse (1977b).

Obviously a difficulty with patterned reinforcement is building the script and making it contingent upon appropriate behaviors. Because interviewers cannot really tell when respondents are being accurate or complete, there is a certain amount of guessing about when to reinforce and when not. The message is indirect and must be inferred by the respondent at best. Moreover, inadvertently, interviewers may be reinforcing erroneous reporting. Three other approaches designed by Cannell and his associates, designed to attack the same problem, produce similar results and may be easier to use on a routine basis.

Modeling

Hensen (1973) reasoned that the best way to communicate to respondents about how they were expected to perform was to give them a demonstration. He produced a tape recording of a respondent who verbally exhibited an extraordinary amount of concern about being accurate and complete. Interviewers played this tape recording at the beginning of the interview, to "show the respondent what an interview was like," then proceeded to do the interviews. In a controlled test of the efficacy of this procedure, there was some evidence that the modeling improved the quality of reporting.

Standardized Instructions

Having an interviewer read a set of instructions to the respondent before the interview is probably the most straightforward way of trying to make sure that interviewers set the same high standards for all respondents. One set of instructions tested by Cannell reads as follows:

It is very important that your answers be accurate and complete. Please take your time. Feel free to ask me questions if there is any point at which you are not clear what is wanted.

The interviewer then proceeds with the interview. Again, Cannell et al. (1977b) demonstrated that these instructions have a salutary effect on reporting. This treatment seems to be particularly effective with better educated respondents.

Commitment

The preceding three treatments, reinforcement, modeling, and instructions, all attack the problem of standardized goals for the respondent by making sure that the interviewer communicates, more or less directly, the fact that accuracy and complete reporting are the appropriate standards. However, there is nothing active on the part of the respondent in any of these treatments; it is simply a matter of making sure the interviewer is heard, that the message is the correct one, and that all interviewers deliver the same message. Cannell devised another strategy designed to get respondents more actively committed to good performance.

The treatment he tested worked as follows: After obtaining initial agreement from a respondent to conduct an interview, the interviewer asked a few questions "so that the respondent could get an idea of what was involved." Then the interviewer asked for a commitment. Respondents were told that accurate and complete answers were critical to this research. The respondent was to agree to try as hard as he or she could to answer the questions accurately. In the initial tests, respondents were asked to sign a form committing themselves to complete and accurate answers to the extent possible. In later tests, respondents were simply asked for a verbal commitment. With either treatment, the respondent was told that if he or she would not make a commitment, the interview was over.

Cannell fully expected a good number of respondents to resist committing themselves. He thought the rates of refusal would skyrocket. This was not the case. Only 2 or 3% of those who initially agreed to be interviewed failed to continue with the survey, and there are several tests that show that such commitment improves respondents' performance. This would seem to be the ultimate treatment, making expectations clear and having the respondent actively buy into the set of expectations.

Table 4.7 shows the combined effect of three of these strategies—instructions, reinforcement (feedback), and commitment on the number of health events reported in a telephone survey. It can be seen that the experimental procedures clearly induce people to report more health events (Cannell et al., 1987). Since underreporting has been documented as the main type of error for several of these estimates, a case can be made that the higher estimates are very likely to be better estimates.

Cannell et al. (1977b) report data that are less equivocal that the experimental treatments produce "better" respondent performance. For example, respondents were more likely to report an exact data of a doctor visit, rather than the month or a range, under experimental conditions. They were also more likely to check records to ensure the accuracy of their reporting when exposed to the experimental procedures.

CONCLUSION

In this chapter we have considered three aspects of the way the interview is set up by the interviewer: the reasons respondents participate in surveys, the way the interviewer-respondent relationship is structured, and the standards that are set for performing the interview task. Of these three, there is no doubt that the way the interviewer sets standards for respondent performance is both the most important source of between-interviewer variation that can be related to interviewer effects on data and also the most important opportunity for increasing standardization of surveys and reducing bias in survey estimates.

There is great diversity among respondents in what they know about the purposes of surveys in which they participate. Although interviewers differ in the extent to which they try to provide background information to respondents, the effect of these interviewer differences on how much respondents actually absorb about the study is not well documented. There is reason to think that most respondents get about as much information as they want or need in order to justify a decision to participate.

There is one study that indicates the possibility that more information does have a positive effect on the quality of reporting of well educated respondents (Cannell et al., 1968). There is a possibility that doing a better job of informing respondents about research projects might improve the quality of data collection; that is a topic worthy of additional research. At this point, our practical prescriptive advice is to make sure that interviewers are equipped with an accurate set of answers to commonly asked questions, and that they give respondents an opportunity to ask the questions on their

Table 4.7

Percent of Persons in Selected Response Categories
by Experimental Interview Treatment

Response Category	Experimental Interview Treatment	
	Control form	Experimental form
	Percent with 1 or more in past 2 weeks	
Bed days	7.3%	10.0%*
Work loss days	6.3	8.8 *
Cut–down days	8.4	11.5 *
Dentist visits	6.8	7.4
Doctor visits	17.4	17.5
Acute conditions	14.9	17.7 *
	Percent with 1 or more in past 12 months	
Doctor visits	72.6	74.5
Hospital episodes	13.4	12.5 *
	Percent with 1 or more	
Chronic conditions	29.2	35.8 *
Limitation of activity	20.4	27.6 *
	Number	
Approximate size of sample	4,217	3,993

SOURCE: Adapted from Cannell et al. (1987).
NOTE: Experimental treatment used a combination of instructions, feedback and commitment procedures.
*Difference between control and experimental forms significant at $p < 0.05$.

minds, so that respondents do not go into interviews with less information than they want.

The guidelines with respect to the quality of the interviewer-respondent relationship are similarly sketchy. Although interviewers differ in the extent to which they are naturally reserved, there is virtually no documentation that one interviewer's personal style is better than another's. Enough attention to the interpersonal aspects of the interview to put the respondent at ease is probably useful, but Weiss (1968) and Hensen (1973) report data that suggest an interpersonal style is likely, if anything, to be counterproductive. Probably a predominantly professional style, one which is businesslike, is the right general orientation.

Finally, there is strong evidence that interviewers differ significantly in the extent to which they ask respondents to work at being good, accurate reporters. Almost certainly, that is one of the differences among interviewers that most affects data and reduces the quality of data. Cannell and his associates have successfully intervened in the reporting process by changing the ways that interviewers communicate goals and standards. All the facts converge to make this one of the most important and promising paths to standardization and improved data quality.

Interestingly, although these techniques have been in the literature for over a decade, they are not widely used in the survey research field. Admittedly it is not easy to design a reinforcement schedule. However, to build in standardized instructions which set standards at the beginning of the interview is not difficult. Moreover, asking respondents for a verbal commitment is not hard and has been shown to be feasible and effective on the telephone, as well as in person.

Standardized instructions, asking for verbal commitments to performance, and insisting that interviews be conducted at a slow pace, are straight-forward ways to help the interviewers set standards. Our strong feeling is that most survey enterprises would benefit and produce better quality data if they were part of their standard operating procedures.

5

The Role of Question Design
in Standardized Interviewing

One of the most important ways for a researcher to ensure standardized interviewing is to give interviewers questions that can be easily asked and answered. In Chapter 3, we discussed the techniques that interviewers are taught that help them handle questions in a standardized way. In Chapters 6 through 8, we will discuss the options available to researchers to increase the odds that interviewers will do what they are told to do. In this chapter we focus on improving the questionnaire itself, because the better the interview schedule, the better the interviewing.

In any survey, the questions will exhibit a range in the extent to which interviewers affect the answers they obtain. Figure 5.1 graphically represents the distribution of intraclass correlations for the 130 items in our study of interviewer effects. Others have published similar distributions from theirs and others' studies (Groves and Magilavy, 1980). The distributions varied from study to study depending on the quality of interviewing and the content and quality of the survey instrument but all were basically similar to our distribution. At the moment, we are less interested in why the distributions vary than we are in the fact that some questions are more affected by interviewers than others.

The focus of this chapter is to describe the characteristics of those questions that are at the high end of the distribution, that are most affected by interviewers. We examined a number of ideas that have been explored in the research literature. Our answer will not be surprising, given what we have said up to this point: *interviewer effects are likely to be highest for those questions for which interviewers must exercise discretion and judgment in order to obtain an adequate answer.*

QUESTION CONTENT

On the surface, it seems quite plausible that the content of a question would affect the extent to which interviewers influence the answers. Two

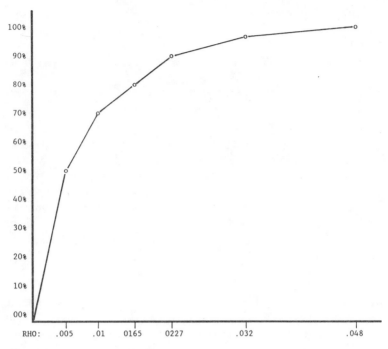

Figure 5.1. Cumulative Distribution of *Rho* for 130 Survey Items

aspects of question content seem particularly plausible: the sensitivity of a question and whether a question asks about attitudes and opinions or about facts.

It is well documented that material that is likely to be sensitive or embarrassing tends to be underreported in surveys. Locander et al. (1976), for example, showed that bankruptcy and arrest for drunken driving were reported at very low rates, despite the fact that they were unlikely to be forgotten. Cannell et al. (1965d, 1965a, 1977a) showed that hospitalizations associated with diagnoses that were likely to be threatening or embarrassing were reported at lower rates than others. Our issue, however, is somewhat different. It is not how well such events are reported in the absolute but, rather, the extent to which the measurement is consistent across interviewers. It does seem reasonable to think that some interviewers would be more successful than others in establishing a kind of relationship with a respondent in which sensitive material would be reported. However, there is very little, if any, empirical evidence to support that hypothesis.

The most support we have seen is reported by Sudman, Bradburn, Blair, and Stocking (1977). They found that interviewer expectations about whether a question would be troublesome or sensitive to respondents was related to the likelihood that they would get an adequate answer to the question. Interviewers who thought a question would be sensitive to respondents were less likely to get an answer at all. With respect to the substantive answers that were obtained, however, Sudman did not find significant interviewer effects distinctively associated with the questions he (or the interviewers) thought were likely to be more sensitive or embarrassing.

In our own research, we coded a series of questions by how likely it was that the answers would be sensitive and embarrassing and looked at the relationship to intraclass correlations. We found no significant association with the coded sensitivity of the questions; in fact, if anything, the intraclass correlations were lower for items rated as sensitive. So, while the theory seems compelling, there is no research evidence to support the notion that sensitive material is harder to measure in a standardized way than nonsensitive items.

Kish (1962) explored the hypothesis that attitudinal or opinion questions were more likely to be influenced by interviewers than questions about factual material. The argument is that questions about facts (past events or current situations that can be independently verified) are rooted in some kind of objective reality. Questions about attitudes and opinions, in contrast, cannot be verified or observed by anyone other than the respondent. To the extent that someone thinks that the source of interviewer error is either that interviewers influence respondents to change answers or that respondents alter their answers to fit interviewer expectations, it is a sensible hypothesis that answers about attitudes and opinions might be more susceptible to such changes than answers about objective events.

As plausible as that hypothesis seems, again, the data are lacking to support that theory. Kish's data did not indicate any differences between attitudinal and factual data from the point of view of interviewer effects. Our own research also failed to find a significant difference in the extent to which interviewers affected attitudinal and factual answers. Overall, we found factual questions were slightly more affected by interviewers than opinion questions.

That generalization was not true for all classes of opinion items, however. Opinion items that were rated especially difficult to answer, generally because respondents were unlikely to have well developed opinions on the topic, did turn out to be significantly affected by interviewers. However, we are confident that the explanation lies less with the content than with other characteristics of those questions which will be discussed below.

Overall, there is nothing in the research literature to support the generalization that the subject of a question has any consistent bearing on whether or not the researcher can design a standardized measurement procedure.

QUESTION FORM

One of the most obvious differences in question form is whether the respondent is given a set of answers from which to choose (a closed or fixed response question) or is asked to answer in his or her own words (an open-ended question). The latter type of question offers more potential for interviewer effect both because of possible ambiguity of what kind of answer will suffice and because interviewers have a more difficult recording task.

There are several kinds of interviewer-related error reported in the research literature that pertain primarily to open-ended questions. For example, Hyman et al. (1954) reported that interviewers tended to selectively probe ambiguous answers based on their perceptions of the respondent's "real position"; they also found errors in recording answers reflecting a tendency for interviewers to leave out points that were inconsistent with their sense of the main position of the respondent. Neither of these errors is pertinent to fixed-response questions.

When looking at intraclass correlations, Groves and Magilavy (1980) report that the number of codable answers given, including the likelihood of giving no codable answer at all, was highly correlated with the interviewer. Again, that only is an issue for open-ended questions.

In our own research, however, when we compared intraclass correlations for large samples of open versus fixed-response questions, we found no statistically significant difference. Although there was some evidence that open-ended questions were more likely to be problematic, it was not a statistically stable trend.

THE QUESTION-AND-ANSWER PROCESS

After concluding that we could not produce generalizations about the quality of questions as standardized measures simply from observing their characteristics, we decided we had to study the interaction between interviewer and respondent in more detail. We took 100 tape recorded interviews done by 57 interviewers and developed a detailed code about what happened between the interviewer and respondent in the process of trying to get an answer to the question. Among other things, we counted the frequency with which eight different behaviors occurred that might have some bearing on the measurement process:

1. whether or not the question was read exactly as worded;
2. whether or not the interviewer correctly used a probe to obtain an adequate answer;
3. whether or not an interviewer used a directive probe;
4. whether or not an interviewer failed to probe when a probe was needed to get an adequate answer;
5. (for open-ended questions only) whether or not the interviewer's recording of the answer was an accurate verbatim recording;
6. whether or not an interviewer gave the respondent inappropriate feedback to an answer;
7. whether or not the interviewer engaged in inappropriate interpersonal behavior; and
8. whether or not there was laughter during the question and answer process.

The incidence of each of these behaviors was counted, with careful check coding, for each interaction in the interview. We had previously calculated which questions were and were not subject to significant interviewer effects, as measured by the intraclass correlation coefficient. We then analyzed the interviewer behaviors we had coded to see whether or not certain kinds of behavior could differentiate between the questions that interviewers did influence and those that they did not. These findings are shown in Table 5.1.

Inappropriate feedback or interpersonal behavior did not occur at a high rate per question, and that may explain why it did not show up as a correlate of individual question results. This does not mean that interpersonal behavior does not affect the quality of the data, but among trained interviewers such behavior does not explain why certain individual questions are more or less likely to be affected by interviewers.

We thought that questions that were frequently reworded or misread by interviewers would be those most affected by interviewers. This was not the case. Across all questions, whether or not interviewers read the questions exactly as worded was not correlated with the size of interviewer effect.

We did find other aspects of the interaction that were correlated with interviewer effects. The major correlate of interviewer effects was the extent to which a question required probing. All three of the probing counts, the number of correct probes, the number of directive probes, and the number of occasions when the interviewer failed to probe, were associated with the size of the intraclass correlation. Basically when a question routinely requires probing, it produces an opportunity for interviewers to make mistakes. Every time a question requires a probe, it gives the interviewer a chance to use a directive probe rather than a nondirective probe; it gives the interviewer an opportunity to fail to probe an answer that requires probing. Moreover, such decisions affect the data in ways that can be associated with the interviewer.

The other correlate of the interviewer-related intraclass correlation was the likelihood that interviewers would make a recording error. Although such errors were considerably less common across all survey items than probing errors, our findings were consistent with Hyman et al.'s (1954) conclusion that selective recording is a significant contributor to non-standardized measurement across interviewers.

We have reviewed the research literature and looked in more detail at the interviewer-respondent interactions in our own work to see if we could understand the kinds of question features that required probing, and whether or not there were specific kinds of situations that were distinctively likely to produce interviewer effects. We consider this an important area for ongoing research and do not think our answers are definitive yet. However, we have identified some question characteristics that appear likely to produce interviewer effects on data.

CORRELATES OF PROBING

Although our studies of question characteristics did not lead us to identify any broad classifications of questions that routinely are more affected by interviewers than others, there are some generalizations about question types that are more likely to require probing, which in turn are more likely to be subject to interviewer effects (see Table 5.2). Specifically, open-ended questions are much more likely to require probing than are closed-ended questions. There also is a tendency for questions about opinions, rather than facts, and questions that were judged by raters to be more difficult than average for respondents to answer (either because they involved a potentially difficult recall task or required formulating an opinion about something respondents were unlikely to have thought about before) to be more likely to require probing. Also, difficult questions and questions about opinions were likely to elicit directive probes.

Hence, our generalization is not that any one of these types of questions (difficult, open-ended, or opinion) is in and of itself distinctively suscepti-

Table 5.1

Significant Correlations Between the Incidence of
Specific Interviewer Behaviors and *Rho*

Interviewer Behavior	Correlation with Rho
Laughing	—
Incorrect reading of question	—
Correct probe	.23
Directive probe	.20
Failed to probe	.49
Inappropriate feedback on answer	—
Inappropriate interpersonal behavior	—
Incomplete or inaccurate verbatim recording on open q's	.39

NOTE: Cells with dashes showed nonsignificant correlations, p < .05. Correlations are based on coding of behaviors while asking 65 items for 100 different interviews. Degrees of freedom = 64.

ble to interviewer effects. However, they are distinctively likely to require interviewer probing, and to the extent that is the case, they are less likely to be standardized measures.

SPECIFIC THREATS TO STANDARDIZED MEASUREMENT

Identifying questions that routinely require probing can be done with reliability by tape recording and coding interviewer-respondent interactions.

Table 5.2

Significant Correlations Between the Incidence of
Specific Interviewer Behaviors and Question Characteristics

Interviewer Behavior	Question Characteristics			
	Difficult	Sensitive	Opinion	Open
Laughing	.34	—	.31	.35
Incorrect reading of question	.52	—	.45	—
Correct probe	.34	—	.24	.63
Directive probe	.59	—	.57	.48
Failed to probe	.28	−.22	.38	.56
Inappropriate feedback on answer	.29	—	.27	.42
Inappropriate interpersonal behavior	.28	—	.24	.23
Incomplete or inaccurate verbatim recording on open q's	.28	−.26	.38	.59

NOTE: Cells with dashes showed nonsignificant correlations, p. < .05. Correlations are based on coding of behaviors while asking 65 items for 100 different interviews. Degrees of freedom = 64.

However, we have also identified at least five kinds of question properties that may be identified by simple pretest procedures that have been found by us or others to increase the likelihood of significant interviewer effects. These are:

1. Number of points mentioned;
2. The hidden screening question;
3. Unclear terms in question;
4. Unclear response expectations; and
5. Field coded answers.

Number of Points

Most often, it is an open-ended opinion question in which the number of different responses given by a respondent affects the data.

Example: What are the things you like best about living in this neighborhood?

The question permits the respondent to give multiple answers. The fact that there is a plural word, "things," would indicate to most interviewers that they should probe at least once to try to get a second response. However, the question is unclear to respondents and interviewers about how many answers or points is enough. As noted previously, Groves and Magilavy (1980) reported that the number of different points made by respondents was one of the characteristics of answers that is most affected by interviewers. Anytime the researcher does not specify what is expected, there will be inconsistency across interviewers.

The Hidden Screening Question

The following are examples of hidden screening questions:

1. What is the best book you read last year?
2. For whom do you think you will be voting in the next election—Harry Truman or Thomas Dewey?
3. What is the best thing that happened to you yesterday, the event that pleased you most?

All three of the above questions, and many other questions that are asked by survey researchers, include at least two questions at once. One of the questions is a hidden question about whether or not the main question actually applies to the respondent.

> **Analysis:** The first question assumes that the respondent has read at least one book (but actually to answer the comparative question, two or more books would be better) during the past year. The respondent might be able to say that the question does not make any sense, and does not apply, because no books were read. A respondent, further, might be able to reject answering the question because none of the books read were liked. Although in theory one can choose a favorite book among unliked books, there is reason to wonder if the question applies in those circumstances.
>
> The voting question includes hidden questions about whether or not the respondent plans to vote, and probably more importantly, whether or not the respondent has made a choice or has an idea about which candidate to support. That one question is really a series of three questions which include whether or not the respondent is planning to vote, whether or not he has a current preference between the two candidates, and then what that preference is.
>
> The question about what was the best thing that happened yesterday is technically a correct question: No matter how terrible things were yesterday, there must have been a best thing. However, if a respondent does not think anything happened that "pleased" him, then he may want to give the answer "nothing." Again, interviewers and respondents may actually treat the one question as two questions: "Was there anything that happened yesterday that pleased you or gave you pleasure?" Then: "What was it?"

These issues are variations on the "don't know" problem. For almost any question, there is the possibility that a respondent will say he does not have the information or has not given the question enough thought to give an appropriate answer.

From a standardization point of view, of course, the problem is that there are no rules or procedures written into the questions to handle the hidden question. The hidden question is not asked explicitly. Interviewers have to decide how to handle the situation when the respondent volunteers an answer to the hidden question, the one that was not explicitly asked but was assumed, which means that the main question does not apply. As is often the case when the procedures are not spelled out, interviewers handle the situation inconsistently. Studies have shown that the rates at which interviewers accept answers such as "don't know" or "does not apply" vary markedly. In addition, Schuman and Presser (1981) show that the handling of these "don't know" answers has a substantive effect on the distribution of answers.

Poorly Defined Terms

In our research, we thought questions that included terms that were not well defined would be distinctively prone to interviewer effects. We had raters code questions as to whether or not they included "ambiguous" terms. Although we did not have as large a sample of such questions as we would have liked, we found no evidence of a relationship between a question being so rated and the size of the interviewer associated intraclass correlation.

Nonetheless, when we studied interactions between interviewers and respondents in detail, it was clear that some significant interviewer effects stemmed from nonstandardized conversations about the meanings of key terms. We have since come to conclude that only certain types of ambiguities cause problems for standardization.

A key observation was that ambiguous terms did not consistently lead to probing. Some terms and questions were ambiguous, their meaning unclear, but they were not problematic for respondents. For example, respondents were asked how many days they had eaten breakfast in the preceding seven days. We are absolutely certain that respondents differed in what they considered breakfast to be. However, "breakfast" is a term that respondents think they understand, whether or not they define it the same as other respondents or as the researcher. Hence, while it was not a clear term from a measurement perspective, this question did not lead to unstandardized interactions between interviewers and respondents.

We think that a question that includes ambiguities that can appropriately be dealt with by simply repeating the question will probably produce a standardized measurement process. Of course, all questions will be better if they are consistently understood across respondents and if the respondents and researcher share the same view of what the question means. Questions produce response error if they are not clear, but the error is not related to the interviewer unless the question stimulates interaction between the respondent and interviewer, which in turn provides the interviewer with an opportunity to be inconsistent. If interviewers know how to behave and what to do when asked a question about a question, there will not be inconsistency.

The problems occur, then, when an appropriate interviewer response is not simply to reread the question or not to say, in response to a question about the meaning of a term, "whatever it means to you."

Below are two examples of questions from our research which show high interviewer effects that we think suffered from this problem. The ambiguous term is highlighted with italics.

1. How long ago was the last time you were actually seen by a *doctor* for your health—within the last month, 1 to 6 months ago, 6 months to a year ago, or more than a year ago?

2. In the past 12 months did you have *eczema* or *psoriasis*?

In question 1, the ambiguity is what counts as a visit to a doctor; in question 2, the meaning of eczema or psoriasis is not familiar to all respondents.

In each case, the question wording itself does not deal with the uncertainty, yet it clearly does not make sense to ignore a respondent plea for clarification. The result was a nonstandardized interaction between interviewers and respondents on some occasions, which led to high interviewer effects.

Unclear Response Expectations

A particularly important kind of ambiguity associated with interviewer effects is when the question wording does not specify what constitutes an adequate response. In one sense, a special case of this is the issue discussed above, the number of responses required or expected to an open-ended question. However, as we studied question interactions, we found other instances of this same kind of phenomenon that are perhaps more general.

"From what source would you say you get the most information about health and what you should do to keep healthy?"

Although on the surface that may seem to be a reasonable question, it turned out to pose two problems for respondents and interviewers. First, there was some concern about what constitutes a "source." There are processes whereby people acquire information, such as talking with people or reading or watching television. Do those constitute sources, or are they only conduits of information from some other source?

Then there is the related question of how specific one needs to be. For example, is "from reading" an adequate answer. If not, is greater specificity required about the sort of thing one is reading (magazines, books, newspapers) or is the source the issue (articles in the *New England Journal of Medicine*, Ann Landers, my horoscope).

There is absolutely no help in the question wording to deal with these issues. Consequently, the opportunities for interviewer discretion, and hence inconsistency, are abundant. First, interviewers get to decide whether or not an answer is detailed and specific enough to be adequate. If they decide not, they then have no real tools to help the respondent; so they get to write their own questions to solve the problem.

Field Coded Questions

We have a real bias against field coded questions, that is, questions which are asked in an open-ended format, but which the interviewer is asked to record by checking boxes. Such questions require interviewers to be coders. Interviewers are not chosen nor trained to be coders; they have lots of other things to do in the interview besides think about coding; and, worst of all, their coding cannot be check coded to detect errors or find out how bad they are at it.

Our own studies included only a few questions that were field coded. On average, they were not significantly worse with respect to interviewer effects than others. However, two of the worst questions in our study were field coded. One was taken verbatim from the National Health Interview Survey. *Why did you go to the doctor the last time you went?* Interviewers were supposed to record answers in one of the following categories:

1. Diagnosis or treatment
2. Check up
3. Pre- or postnatal exam
4. Eye exam
5. Immunization
6. Other (specify)

Another field coded question we made up ourselves. *In what area of your life would you most like to see some changes?* Interviewers were supposed to record answers in one of the following categories:

1. Job
2. Children
3. Finances, money
4. Health
5. Leisure
6. Other (specify)

Not only were the intraclass correlations high for these items, our review of interviewer-respondent interactions show they produced some of the worst (that is, least standardized, most directive) interviewing behavior that we saw in our survey.

The reason, of course, is that we put the interviewer in an absolutely impossible situation. On the one hand, these two questions happen to be distinctively nonspecific about what kind of answers constitute an adequate answer. "Why" questions are always problematic. Consider these possible answers to the question about why did you go to the doctor. "My husband said I should go" or "Because I believe in doctors." Although obviously many respondents figure out in context that the idea is to answer about the medical reason or problem for going to the doctor, there is nothing in the specific wording of the question that helps them get there.

However, the real problem is that the respondent has no idea what distinctions are sitting in front of the interviewer, and the interviewer has been given no standardized strategy for giving clues to the respondent. Respondents give answers that are relatively close to a response category, but not unambiguously so. The interviewer is fairly sure where the answer should go, but interviewers differ in how strictly they adhere to nondirective probing techniques to get the information needed to classify the answer. Moreover, reviewers could hear on the tapes how frustrating it was to interviewers not to be able to get a definitive answer. In the end, some of them would simply say: "So would you say that was a check up?"

There is not clear empirical evidence that field coding is a terrible thing to do under all circumstances. Only under some circumstances. Specifically, field coding may be okay if the kind of answer that meets the question objectives, both in terms of its character and its specificity, is clear from the question that is asked. However, it is a bad way to design questions if the respondent cannot discern from the question what constitutes the range of acceptable answers.

It may be that an open-ended question that does not specify well what answers will meet the question objectives will generate interviewer effects whether it is field coded or not. It may be that other aspects of the question, rather than the field coding itself, lead to interviewer effects. The quality of the coding categories—how clear, how nonoverlapping, how well they fit the range of answers given, how they are formulated—may also affect the interviewers' performance. Nonetheless, we continue to be very conservative about the use of field coding when designing standardized interview schedules.

DESIGNING SURVEY INSTRUMENTS
TO MINIMIZE INTERVIEWER EFFECTS

Designing questions to minimize interviewer effects boils down to building into the question itself what the respondent needs to know in order to answer the question. The idea is to write a question that provides a complete script for the interviewer, everything the interviewer will have to say, so that no idiosyncratic choices about how to clarify the question or how to probe the answers will be needed.

That may not sound profound or insightful. Possibly readers of Stanley Payne's book (1951) would have thought those principles were reasonably stated then. However, significant numbers of survey questions do not meet those standards, and, hence, are handled inconsistently by interviewers. Moreover, in our experience in working with colleagues about question design, we think there is far too little appreciation of the importance of minimizing the need for probing and anticipating within the question wording what kind of information will be needed to achieve question objectives.

Our discussion of question problems suggests some guidelines for improved question design. First, building in good definitions of key terms, particularly when counts of certain classes of events are needed, is sound question design. Interviewers and respondents should not have to cope with questions that lack needed definitions.

Second, there is no doubt that being attentive to hidden screening questions and making them explicit will produce better, more standardized measurement. Although Schuman and Presser (1981) do not explicitly advocate the screening question as better, their data seem compelling to us. Rather than have respondents or interviewers decide whether or not a question applies in their own inconsistent ways, it is better measurement to set up a consistent process for having respondents decide whether or not the question should apply to them. Such design reduces error across respondents.

Third, researchers can reduce interviewer-related error by writing questions that make the response expectations clear. One obvious way to do that is to use closed-response rather than open-ended questions; there is no clearer specification of what responses are appropriate than to say, "pick one of these answers."

When open-ended questions are used, researchers would do well to think about ways in which they could narrow the discretion for interviewers and respondents about the kinds of answers that would count. The adverbial words, how, when, where, why, how much, should almost always be avoided; the kind of answer that is wanted can always be better specified by avoiding one of those words, and interviewers are often forced to rewrite questions in order to get answers in the correct terms (see Table 5.3).

Fourth, interviewer and respondent variability in the number of points they make in response to open-ended questions should be controlled by specifying a number of points to be made. A preference of ours is to ask for the "main reason" rather than "all the reasons," so that each respondent only gives one answer. If multiple answers are really desired, one could

Table 5.3

Adverbial Equivalents

Adverbial Formulation	Alternative Interpretations
1. HOW do you get to work?	a. What kind of transportation do you use to get to work?
	b. By what route do you proceed to work?
2. WHEN did you move to this address?	a. In what year did you . . . .
	b. How many years ago did you . . . .
	c. At what age did you . . . .
3. WHY did you vote for candidate X?	a. What characteristics of candidate X attracted your vote?
	b. What characteristics of candidate Y reduced your willingness to vote for him?
	c. Which interests or concerns of yours were reflected in your vote for candidate X?
4. WHERE did you live when you were a teenager?	a. In which city or town did you live?
	b. With whom were you living?
	c. In what kind of housing structure did you live?
5. HOW MUCH money do you make?	a. How many dollars are you paid?
	b. How does your income compare with that of others?
	c. How does your income compare with your needs?

ask for the second most important reason. The goal is to eliminate interviewer and respondent uncertainty about what the measurement task is so that the researcher, rather than the interviewer or respondent, is making the decisions about what the respondent does in response to the question.

More important than any of these recommendations about particular question design strategies, however, is the need for careful evaluation of questions during the pretest and pilot phases of studies. Our research has shown that we cannot a priori identify classes of questions that are subject to significant interviewer effects. Questions that require a good deal of probing, particularly those where interviewers must go beyond simply repeating the question, in order to meet the question objectives, are most susceptible to interviewer effects. We have found such questions among closed-ended and open questions, among attitudinal and factual questions. However, it is possible to identify many such questions during the pretest phases of research studies. We think identifying questions that generate a high rate of probing and improving them before finalizing the questionnaire is one of the most fruitful ways to reduce interviewer-related error in surveys.

STRATEGIES FOR IDENTIFYING QUESTION PROBLEMS

A typical pretest of a survey instrument consists of experienced interviewers taking 10 to 20 interviews, then meeting for an hour or two with the researchers to discuss any problems they encountered. Although such pretests are useful, we are convinced researchers can and should do much more than that to evaluate their questions. We and others are in the process of designing and evaluating better ways to test questions. DeMaio (1983) and Converse and Presser (1986) provide two of the more thorough reviews of the strategies available for evaluating questions. The following are four steps that we think have considerable potential to improve question design:

1. *Focused discussion groups* are one of the oldest and best ways to begin the design of survey instruments. Groups of six to eight people typical of those to be interviewed should be brought together. Two to four groups are usually enough. The groups should be taken through a discussion of their experiences and thoughts about the areas to be covered in the survey. The availability of low-cost video taping makes it possible for a whole research team to review what is said in the groups without having to be present.

   From the point of view of minimizing interviewer effects, the specific outcomes of such discussions can include identifying terms or concepts that are not consistently understood and need definition, identifying the range of answers people give to potential questions, and identifying false assumptions that might be embedded in questions about the way respondents behave or think about issues to be covered. Such focussed group discussions will improve not only the ability of researchers to design a survey instrument that can be administered in a standardized way but will probably improve the extent to which they ask the questions that will provide the information they need. We believe that almost any survey research project will benefit from several focussed group discussions prior to designing a survey instrument.

2. *Cognitive research techniques* have been newly introduced into the survey research field (e.g., Jabine et al., 1984). For many years cognitive psychologists have been studying how people process information, go about recalling information, and organize their thoughts, but only recently have their techniques been brought to bear on designing better questions in surveys. Their procedures primarily involve relatively intensive, lengthy sessions with a few typical respondents. The technique which seems most widely used at the moment is the so-called "think aloud" interview. In this interview, respondents are asked to talk out loud about their thought processes as they go through a pretest version of a survey instrument. By listening to people talk about how they are understanding and thinking about the questions, researchers can identify ambiguities in what the questions mean and difficulties in the response task.

A variation on this approach is to go through the interview schedule twice. First, a respondent is asked to answer questions as a normal pretest respondent would do. The interviewer then takes the respondent through the same interview schedule again, asking the respondent to discuss and explain answers and any difficulties a respondent had with the questions.

These techniques are still being developed and evaluated. They are quite labor intensive, but obviously they have considerable potential payoff for identifying the kinds of problems that produce error.

3. *Better use of pretest interviews* is another area in which we think there is potential. Although interviewers with experience definitely have the ability to identify some characteristics of questions that will pose problems, our observation is that interviewers vary greatly in what they consider to be a problem. In fact, experienced interviewers tend to be good at solving the problems that researchers pose for them through poor question design, and we often find they are not sensitive to some of the difficulties questions create for them and for their respondents.

We have been exploring the potential of giving interviewers more training in what to look for during a pretest. The goal is to sensitize them to questions that are not easy to read as worded and, in particular, to questions that routinely require probing and clarification in order to obtain adequate answers. We also believe having interviewers complete a standardized, written rating of each question will make their input more systematic and useful. We are still evaluating alternative ways to use interviewers in the question evaluation process, but we are convinced that more attention both to interviewer training and to the debriefing process can improve the ability of interviewers to identify question problems.

4. *Tape recording and coding* pretest interviews is, to our mind, potentially the most important innovation in the evaluation of survey questions. To use this strategy effectively, it is best to take at least 25 pretest interviews in order to increase the stability of measurement. Interviewers tape record interviews with respondent permission; this can be done in person or on the telephone. On the telephone, when the respondent is asked for permission to tape record the interview, be sure the respondent's answer is recorded on the tape.

The tapes can be coded in about twice the time it takes to conduct an interview. The coding scheme that we have been working with requires a coder to count the number of times four or five different behaviors occur for each question: Whether or not the question was read exactly as written, whether or not the respondent asked for clarification, whether the respondent provided an adequate answer after the question was read or whether probing was required. We have used two approaches to the latter:

1. coders count the number of times the interviewer either probes or repeats the question; or

2. coders count the number of times the respondent gives an inadequate or incomplete answer.

We then calculate the rates at which these events occurred; that is, the rates at which questions were misread, the rates at which respondents asked for clarification, the rates at which questions required additional probing or produced inadequate answers.

We are still working on the best way to code these events, the stability of the results, and the most cost effective way to use them as indicators of question quality. However, as indicated in data presented earlier in this chapter, we have evidence that questions that require additional probing are distinctively likely to be subject to interviewer effects. We also are sure that this technique reliably identifies questions that are difficult to read as worded. Although we expect to do further work and document the value of these activities, our work to date has convinced us that coding the interaction between interviewers and respondents with a particular eye to indications of difficulty of administering questions in a standardized way, provides meaningful, reliable clues to question problems that can and should be improved before they are put into the field for a full-scale survey.

CONCLUSION

In the next three chapters, we will talk about ways to get interviewers to do what we want them to do during the interview. However, it will be seen that there are limits to researchers' abilities to control interviewers.

As we said early in this chapter, in the studies which are published of interviewer effects on data, between one quarter and one third of the questions were subject to significant interviewer-related error. Moreover, almost certainly, the studies reported in that literature represent the high end of the continuum in terms of interviewer training and attention to methodological detail.

Although having interviewers who are able and willing to do standardized, nondirective interviews is one part of the process of error reduction, the task that they are given also plays an important role on how well they will be able to meet the goals of standardized interviewing. In our studies, we have found that some questions pose virtually impossible tasks for respondents and interviewers; the interviewers simply cannot use the words provided to meet the objectives of the question. Under those circumstances, interviewers have no choice but to write their own scripts. Sometimes that simply means innovations about which probes to use, and how often to use them. Sometimes it means completely writing new questions, developing free-lance explanations or instructions to respondents about what the question means in order to make the task manageable. Whatever the effort, when interviewers start doing that, they do it idiosyncratically, and the result is interview-related error. As others before have concluded, most notably Bradburn and Sudman (1979), one of the best courses to reducing interviewer effects on data is to write better questions; the critical step in writing better questions is careful, thorough development and pretesting procedures before a survey begins.

6

Interviewer Selection and Interviewer-Related Error

What characteristics should one look for in choosing an interviewer? Our interest in answering this question is dependent on to what extent, if any, the characteristics of interviewers are associated with the quality of data they collect.

There are three bases for thinking that interviewer characteristics might affect data. First, some interviewers may be better able than others to carry out the question-and-answer process. Second, certain interviewer characteristics may alter the context or meaning of questions. Third, interviewer characteristics may affect the quality of the relationship between the interviewer and respondent. In this chapter we discuss the evidence regarding these possibilities.

INTERVIEWER CHARACTERISTICS AND PERFORMANCE

There are some interviewer characteristics that are necessary, if not sufficient, to be a good interviewer. The most obvious are good reading and writing skills. In the United States, relatively few professional interviewers are hired who have not finished high school. Although some survey organizations specify a preference for college experience, we are aware of no systematic studies that have associated level of formal education of interviewers with the quality of data they collect.

Sudman and Bradburn (1974) did an extensive meta-analysis, looking at the characteristics of interviewing staffs and the extent to which they could be associated with the quality of data that resulted. The only pattern they identified was that studies using very young interviewers seemed to produce more error. Sudman was pretty sure this finding was an artifact, stemming from the fact that studies using college students tended to be more informal survey studies and that student interviewers often received little training and had no prior interviewing experience.

There have been various efforts to correlate scores on personnel inventories and questionnaires with interviewer performance. Although individual studies have come up with suggestive relationships, as almost any such study would, our reading of the literature is that there are no well documented relationships between interviewer characteristics as measured by any standard test and their ability to carry out the question-and-answer process on a general-purpose, population survey.

One question that is raised from time to time is whether or not special training in the substantive area of a research study should be a requirement for interviewers. Such an issue is most often raised when interviews are to be conducted with professionals in some field. For example, one can propose that lawyers be interviewed by law students, physicians interviewed by nurses or medical students or, more generally, that health interviews be carried out by nurses.

We want to dissociate here the issue of effective enlistment of cooperation from effective conduct of the interview. We are aware of evidence, generally anecdotal and uncontrolled, that cooperation rates have been improved when contact is made by people who appear to be peers or colleagues. These anecdotes say, for instance, that police officers are more likely to respond to research when contact is made by an interviewer who has law enforcement experience. However, with respect to the quality of data collected during an interview, we know of no basis for saying that a specialized background is an asset to an interviewer in carrying out a standardized interview. In fact, while the usual finding is no difference, many experienced survey researchers think that professional interviewers, without specialized background or training in a subject area, will do a better job of interviewing.

This conclusion is hard to document, because it is unusual for the quality of training and supervision of interviewers with special backgrounds to be the same as the usual pool of interviewers. However, it appears that when, for example, law students interview lawyers, they are less likely to probe ambiguous answers, they are more likely to assume they know what the respondent means when the respondent has not been clear, either because "jargon" with which they are familiar seems clear to them, when it is not, or because they are reluctant to probe when they do not completely understand an answer. Interviewers who incorrectly assume they know what the respondent has to say will err by either failing to probe or probing directively. A general interviewer, with no illusion to maintain of expertise or knowledge in the field, may feel free to probe nondirectively until answers are clear.

Sometimes, people carrying out surveys want to collect data in two ways, supplementing data obtained by questions and answers with observations or ratings that require specialized knowledge. For example, a study of needs for support services among the elderly might include some kind of clinical assessments that nurses would be distinctively well qualified to make. In our experience, if one is trying to produce standardized measurement by observation, a researcher will probably be best served by designing measurement procedures that any qualified interviewer can do. It has been demonstrated, moreover, that the usual staff of professional interviewers can be trained to reliably take blood pressures, perform tests of physical mobility, and do a variety of other tasks besides interviewing (e.g., McKinlay et al., 1982).

There may be grounds other than the quality of interviewing on which one would want to choose an interviewer with a specialized background. However, on the basis of the quality of the data gathered in the interview, there is no basis in the research literature for requiring a substantive background on the part of interviewers.

INTERVIEWER CHARACTERISTICS
AND THE CONTEXT OF THE INTERVIEW

The goal of standardized data collection is to have interviewers offer a consistent stimulus. Although interviewers can be trained to ask questions as worded and probe nondirectively, obviously they enter an interview situation with a set of characteristics that cannot be hidden. In person, a respondent can readily discern an interviewer's age, gender, and racial background; also such characteristics as level of education, social class, and ethnic and religious background may be inferred. On the telephone, there is less opportunity for respondent observation, but gender is clearly discernible, and many other characteristics may be inferred, accurately or inaccurately, from the interviewer's name, accent, intonation, and verbal style.

From a practical point of view, it is impossible to assemble an interviewing staff without variation in demographic characteristics if more than one interviewer is going to be used. Moreover, it is easy to think that it is the similarities or differences between the respondents' and interviewers' characteristics that are most critical. Hence, the significance of being a 45 year old interviewer may be different if the respondent is 20, 45, or 75.

The hope for standardization of the measurement process is that such interviewer characteristics are irrelevant and do not affect the answers that are obtained. It is perfectly plausible to think that an interviewer's age, race, or sex would not have any effect on the answers to most questions. Moreover, that turns out to be true. Despite considerable research effort over 40 years to relate interviewer demographic characteristics to the answers they have obtained, there are comparatively few instances when such associations have been found.

Before we begin to summarize the findings, however, it should be pointed out that it is relatively hard to carry out conclusive studies of interviewer demographic characteristics. The vast majority of interviewers used in social science research in the United States are white females who have completed at least 4 years of high school education. In order to study the effects of interviewer race, gender, or education on answers, it usually is necessary to put together a special interviewing staff. Newly trained staffs are seldom as satisfactory as staffs of experienced interviewers. Experienced staffs benefit from the attrition over time that gets rid of a certain number of people who are less suited to the interviewing task. Moreover, the pools of potential interviewers who are male, minority group members, or have not completed high school are comparatively limited, and those that are available may be different in ways that are hard to define. For these and other reasons, there is a problem in disassociating the effects of interviewer demographic characteristics from differences due to experience, training, or interests.

Religion or Ethnicity

One of the earliest and most carefully done studies on this topic looked at the relationship between the apparent Jewishness of the interviewer and respondent answers that might reflect prejudice against Jews or anti-Semitism. Interviewers were sorted into three groups: group one consisted of interviewers who had last names that were considered to be distinctively Jewish and were rated as being Jewish in appearance; group two interviewers had distinctive Jewish names, but were not distinctively Jewish in appearance; group three interviewers had neither distinctive Jewish names nor appearance. These three groups of interviewers were assigned to interview comparable samples. Although the distributions of many items were unaffected by the apparent Jewishness of the interviewer, the answers to questions most directly related to feelings about Jews showed the expected effect: the more clearly identifiable the interviewer was as being Jewish, the less likely respondents were to give answers that appeared to reflect anti-Jewish sentiments (Robinson & Rohde, 1946).

Race

Hyman et al. (1954) report a study of the effect of race of interviewer on the responses of black respondents in 1942. On a series of questions related to the racial situation and intergroup relations as well as the war effort, black respondents in Memphis, Tennessee, gave significantly different answers to white interviewers than to black interviewers. Hyman et al. interpreted the difference as reflecting a pattern of blacks giving the white interviewers the "answers they wanted to hear." A comparable experiment in New York at the same time produced much less dramatic differences. Hyman interpreted his data as showing that race of interviewer was a very important part of the stimulus for such questions in the South in the early 1950's, but was less so in the North, either because Northern black respondents were less likely to stereotype interviewers by race or because Northern respondents were more willing to express their feelings to a white interviewer.

In the 1960's, Schuman and Converse (1971) studied the same issue. Students in the Detroit Area Study course, a survey training course for graduate students in the Department of Sociology, were divided by race and interviewed comparable samples of black and white respondents in Detroit. One strength of this study was that for the most part, black and white interviewers had similar backgrounds in interviewing. The shortcoming was that neither group had extensive training or any experience.

For the vast majority of items in the survey, well over 90%, there was no significant effect of interviewer race on the answers that were obtained. Even questions about general societal issues related to race relations, such as the importance of integrating schools, were unaffected by interviewer race. However, when questions were asked that involved expressing direct feelings or opinions about a racial group, the race of the interviewer mattered. Respondents (both white and black) were less likely to express opinions that suggested critical or negative opinions of the group represented by the interviewer.

In addition, there were a few answers where differences were obtained that did not fit that generalization and that appeared, instead, to be cognitive in origin. For example, one of the largest differences found was that black respondents when asked for their favorite entertainers more frequently mentioned black entertainers when their interviewer was black. This pattern may reflect a shaping of responses to what is perceived to be the interviewer's taste, but the authors also think black respondents may have been stimulated to think of more black entertainers when the interviewer was black (a kind of context effect).

A recent study by Anderson et al. (1988a, 1988b) compared the answers of comparable samples of black respondents to black and white interviewers to questions about voting, then validated the accuracy of answers against voting records. Anderson found that race of interviewer did affect answers: blacks were more likely to tell black interviewers that they planned to vote when interviewed before the election and that they did vote when interviewed after the election. The record check showed the post-election reports to white interviewers were more accurate; respondents over-reported voting to black interviewers. The fact that race of interviewer markedly changed the stimulus situation in this interview is further documented by the fact that respondents interviewed by black interviewers before the election were also distinctively likely to actually vote; the interview altered their behavior.

In the Schuman and Converse study, it was not possible to tell which interviewer obtained the true or best answers. When one is measuring subjective phenomena, there is no way to determine what is the true answer. What is clear is that in a standardized measurement process answers should not be related to some interviewer characteristic. The fact that interviewer race can predict answers means that the measurement is not standardized across race of interviewers. When answers are significantly affected by interviewer race, measurement error would be reduced if interviewers were all of the same race.

INTERVIEWER-RESPONDENT RELATIONSHIPS

The demographic characteristics of the interviewer have been shown to have some predictable effects on the relationship that develops between the respondent and an interviewer: mutual attraction and the extent to which the relationship is interpersonal rather than task oriented. The significance of those effects for the quality of data collected are less clear.

Social Status and Education

Some light on this topic comes from Fowler's (1966) study of the effect of respondent education on the way interviewers and respondents felt about one another during a health interview and how they interacted. There is a body of evidence in the social psychological literature that makes predictions about how the relative status of respondents and interviewers will affect their relationship. In general, people prefer to relate up, to interact with those of the same or higher status, compared to relating with those of lower status. When there are status differences, lower status people prefer to be less task oriented in trying to relate to higher status people, while those with higher status prefer to be task oriented in relating to those with lower status (e.g., Cohen, 1958). One would expect a mutual positive relationship to be most likely to occur when respondents and interviewers are similar in status and in other respects (e.g., Newcomb, 1961 and Lundberg et al., 1949).

Fowler's studies tend to be consistent with this literature. Interviewers were relatively homogeneous with respect to status as reflected in their educational levels, with the majority having finished high school or attended some college. Table 6.1 summarizes a number of relevant findings. In general, it can be seen that when interviewers were asked to rate respondents after an interview, their ratings were directly related to the education of respondents; the higher the respondents' education, the more the interviewer liked them. Moreover, interviewers were significantly more likely to stay after an interview and chat with a respondent if the respondent had finished high school or attended college.

On the respondent's side, there was not a clear monotonic relationship to how well they said they liked the interviewer. However, when asked whether they preferred the interviewer to be businesslike or to visit some, respondents with less education said they preferred "visiting"; those who were just a little below the interviewer in educational level, those with some high school, were most likely to prefer visiting.

Such data would lead one to hypothesize that the best reporting would occur when interviewers and respondents were similar in status. Such thinking at one point encouraged researchers to attempt to recruit staffs of interviewers who were similar in background to respondents when doing studies of people of lower socio-economic status. However, a study by Weiss (1968) casts doubt on the value of such a strategy.

Weiss was studying a sample of welfare mothers in New York. The interview schedule covered a variety of topics, some of which she was able to validate using records. She evaluated the accuracy with which four questions were answered, two having to do with voter registration and voting and two having to do with the performance of children in school. She found that similarity between interviewer and respondent with respect to age, education, and socioeconomic status was not conducive to more valid reporting. There were virtually no instances in which respondent-interviewer pairs that were most similar produced more accurate and less biased data. In contrast, there were a number of instances in which better reporting occurred when the interviewer was distinctively better educated or of a higher socioeconomic status than the respondent.

In Weiss' study, interviewers were also asked to rate the quality of rapport that they had established with respondents. Intriguingly, the higher the "rapport" was rated, the more biased the data that resulted. Weiss's study is one of the most convincing and important on two points: one, that demographic similarity is not a plus for the quality of measurement and; two, that rapport and interpersonal attraction are not necessarily positive, and may have a negative effect on the quality of data in surveys.

Table 6.1

Selected Indicators of Interpersonal Attraction of Interviewer
and Respondent by Education of Respondent

	Education of Respondent			
Indicator of Attraction	*0-8 years grade school*	*1-3 years high school*	*4 years high school*	*1 or more years college*
Interviewer liked respondent "above average"*	54%	55%	66%	73%
Interviewer stayed one or more minutes after interview to talk*	54%	49%	67%	69%
Respondent liked interviewer "very well"	35%	46%	44%	42%
Respondent wanted interviewer to "visit" rather than be "businesslike"*	49%	65%	38%	28%
N	(129)	(89)	(123)	(67)

SOURCE: Adapted from Fowler (1966).

NOTE: *High school graduates different from those with less than 4 years high school by t test, $p < .05$.

In conclusion, there is no basis in the research literature for choosing one interviewer over another based on educational level or social status. If there is a relationship, it probably is complex and may differ from respondent to respondent. Most certainly, there is no basis for choosing a less qualified or less experienced interviewer over a more qualified interviewer in order to get someone who is more similar to the people who are going to be interviewed.

Age of Interviewer

There are not many studies that have systematically looked at interviewer age as a factor in survey responses. Erlich and Reisman (1961) did study the effect of interviewer age on responses given by adolescents. They found differences that were consistent with the hypothesis that older interviewers obtained answers that were more normative, more the sorts of answers that a parent would want to hear. Erlich and Reisman thought that the answers given to younger interviewers, those in their 20's rather than those in their 30's and 40's, may have been more accurate.

One could think of age operating in a way similar to social status, where similarity in age would maximize interpersonal compatibility, and large differences might produce social distance that would potentially formalize the interaction and, possibly, also create a barrier that needs to be overcome. However, Weiss (1968) found no effect of age in her study and to our knowledge there are no studies that demonstrate interviewer-related error associated with interviewer age.

Interviewer Gender

Hyman et al. (1954) report that female respondents gave different answers to male and female interviewers in response to: "No decent man can respect a woman who has sex relations before marriage"; they were significantly more likely to agree when interviewed by a male.

Our own studies also show that there are differences in the way in which respondents rate male and female interviewers. When we re-interviewed respondents to a health survey about their reactions to the interview experience, respondents made 10 different ratings of the way they viewed the interviewer. On all 10 of those ratings, female interviewers were rated more highly by both male and female respondents, many of them to a statistically significant degree. The ratings of friendliness, professionalism, and overall performance are presented in Table 6.2.

Like others, we doubt that we have comparable samples of male and female interviewers. The "pool" of males who are in the market for part-time, temporary work is smaller. Moreover, interviewing may be a job that appeals more to females than to males. Our results are based on only 9 male interviewers. We also should note that these data are based on personal interview experiences in people's homes. The effect of male–female differences may be considerably less for telephone interviews.

We definitely think this is an area that justifies further research. We are extremely reluctant to perpetuate any generalizations across broad groups that are heterogeneous, and certainly interviewer gender is one such broad grouping. Moreover, there is no documentation that these differences indicate female interviewers are collecting better or different data. There is a dearth of credible, well designed studies to examine that hypothesis. However, our data are so clear, we ourselves wonder in the instant kind of relationship that must be established in most survey interviews whether or not gender is an important issue, and we look forward to more data on this topic in the future.

CONCLUSION

For most studies there is no basis for choosing one interviewer over another other than availability and willingness to meet the job requirements.

Table 6.2
Respondent Ratings of Interviewers by Interviewer Gender

Respondent Ratings	Interviewer Gender		
	Male	Female	p
Overall performance of interviewer was "excellent"	44%	62%	< .01
*Interviewer "friendliness" rated a "10"	36%	54%	< .01
*Interviewer "professionalism" rated a "10"	52%	64%	< .05

NOTE: *On scale from 1 to 10, on which 10 is the top.

The relationship between interviewer characteristics and interviewer–related error has seldom been established. However, when the topic of a survey is very directly related to some interviewer characteristic so that potentially a respondent might think that some of the response alternatives would be directly insulting or offensive or embarrassing to an interviewer, researchers may want to think seriously about controlling those characteristics. However, even in the most thorough examination to date of such a situation, (Schuman and Converse's study of black and white answers to black and white interviewers), answers to fewer than 10% of the questions could be significantly associated with interviewer race.

There are so many different interviewer characteristics and behaviors that influence the kind of relationship that is established between an interviewer and a respondent, singling out one characteristic is not productive. From an interviewer-related error point of view, our advice generally is to send out the best, most standardized interviewers that can be found.

However, our studies of the way respondents react to male and female interviewers lead us to wonder whether or not the significance of interviewer gender for responses has been adequately studied. Given our findings, we think it would be surprising if additional effects on the data could not be found as well. However, at this point, such data do not exist. Therefore, for the person concerned with reducing interviewer-related error, the place to focus attention is not on selection but on interviewer training and supervision, topics to which we turn our attention in the next two chapters.

7

Training Interviewers

Virtually no one planning a serious survey would question the value of at least some training for interviewers. The various rules, techniques and procedures for standardized interviewing outlined in the preceding chapters are not so obvious that one could count on interviewers using them on their own. There are, however, numerous questions that could be raised about the optimal or necessary content of training, the techniques to be used in training, and how long training should last.

We take it as a given that for any particular survey, there will be some training required in the specific procedures and objectives of that project. Because data collection tasks vary so greatly in their complexity, it is virtually impossible to generalize about what kind of study specific training is appropriate. For complex interview schedules with complicated definitions and procedures, such as the National Health Interview Survey uses, several days of intensive in-person training is standard and may even be too little to thoroughly familiarize the interviewers with the procedures. In contrast, it is standard practice for national survey organizations merely to mail written material to their trained, experienced interviewers describing the procedures and special complexities of individual projects.

Our focus here, however, is on the initial training of interviewers in the techniques of standardized interviewing, what we would call general interviewer training. Regardless of what is done with respect to training interviewers for a particular survey project, some general orientation to interviewing techniques and procedures will also be necessary.

OPTIONS FOR TRAINING

There are four general parts to the interviewer's job:

1. contacting respondents and enlisting cooperation;
2. establishing a relationship with the respondent;
3. handling the question-and-answer process; and
4. recording the answers.

All of these topics would be covered to some degree in any general interviewer training.

There are several ways in which supervisors can go about teaching people how to be interviewers. They can use:

1. an interviewer manual;
2. lectures;
3. demonstrations;
4. supervised practice; or
5. monitoring performance, with evaluation and feedback, after training is over.

All of the instructional activities that occur prior to taking the first interview that "counts" will be considered training. Arbitrarily, we will consider the monitoring and teaching that goes on after data collection actually begins on a study to be supervision. Supervision is the focus of Chapter 8.

The length of training is obviously highly related to the content and techniques included in training, as well as the cost of training. In academic and government survey organizations, basic interviewer training typically lasts from two to five days, with telephone interviewers generally being trained for a shorter period of time than in-person interviewers. There are many surveys, however, that utilize interviewers who have received less than one day of general interviewing training.

There seem to be at least three issues underlying the differences in the training that interviewers receive. First, some researchers obviously do not believe it makes much difference how interviewers do their jobs. Such a conviction may stem either from a lack of familiarity with research on how interviewers affect data or from having research objectives for which it is judged that a fair amount of error in the measurement can be tolerated.

Second, there is not agreement among professionals about how much training is enough or is beneficial to improve the quality of data. Certainly some researchers feel that a few hours of training is sufficient to get interviewers with reasonable backgrounds to an acceptable level of interviewer performance.

Third, there is a clear relationship between how much training interviewers receive and the conditions under which they work. Organizations training telephone interviewers tend to have shorter training periods, at least in part because they feel they can monitor performance closely, identify problems, and engage in retraining as necessary in a telephone setting. In contrast, personal interviewers usually are much less closely supervised and, hence, supervisors are more likely to want to make sure they are fully prepared before letting them begin to interview.

Most of the balance of this chapter draws on the results of our studies of the way that training and supervision affect interviewers (Fowler and Mangione, 1986). Specifically, in this chapter we examine the way training affects:

1. the interviewers' orientation to the job;
2. the interviewers' skills;
3. the way interviewers relate to respondents and the way respondents react to them; and
4. the quality of data collected.

A STUDY OF THE VALUE OF INTERVIEWER TRAINING

Fifty-seven interviewers, 48 of them females, without previous professional interviewing experience, were recruited and hired. They were systematically assigned to one of four training groups that differed in length and in the kind of learning experiences provided to interviewers. Two of the training programs were designed to replicate common training programs in academic survey organizations, one lasting about two days and the other lasting about five days. Another training program was designed to be the shortest training experience we could design and responsibly send interviewers out to try to interview. It lasted about half a day. The final training program lasted ten days, the goal being to see how much additional benefit could be derived from training that went well beyond conventional standards.

Prior to any of the training programs, interviewers were given a manual and asked to read it. That manual described the skills and techniques that interviewers would be taught. Every effort was made to have the messages be identical across all training programs. The goal was to examine the value of lengthier and more intensive training experiences, not differences in content.

The less-than-one-day training program consisted of a two-hour lecture on interviewing techniques and a demonstration interview.

The two-day training program consisted of the same components as the less-than-one-day program plus a movie on general interviewing techniques, periods of discussion of interviewing procedures, in which interviewers could ask questions, and some supervised practice interviewing.

The five-day training program was similar to the two-day program, except everything was extended: The presentations of techniques were longer, with more opportunity for questions and discussion; there was much more opportunity and emphasis placed on supervised practice, not only going through practice interviews, but also a variety of exercises on individual interviewing skills, such as introducing the study, asking questions, probing, and recording answers.

The ten-day training program had all the components of the five-day training program. In addition, three additional kinds of learning experiences were added. First, the interviewers were trained to evaluate interviewing techniques just as supervisors do on a routine basis at the Center. This was an effort to make them more self conscious and aware of the standards for good interviewing. Second, interviewers read articles about interviewer-related error in surveys; the reader of each article presented the results to the group and the results were discussed. Third, each interviewer went through a short practice interview in someone's home that was observed by a supervisor.

As noted, the content and techniques the interviewers were taught were identical to the other groups, but the extent of the practice and their understanding of the rationale for procedures, as well as their practice in them, was much more extensive than the other groups.

Table 7.1 summarizes the content of the training programs. The main differences between the shortest program and the two-day program was the length of lectures and discussions on interviewing procedures and specific study procedures and the fact that those in the two-day group had 105 minutes of supervised practice, while the shortest group watched a demonstration interview and had no supervised practice. The five-day training program had an extra hour of lecture discussion on interviewing procedures and an extra seven hours of supervised practice compared with the two-day group.

After these training experiences were complete, interviewers were given an assignment of 40 addresses at which to carry out a half-hour health interview. Data about the interviewers' performance came from five different sources:

1. At the end of training, each interviewer took a practice interview which was tape recorded and evaluated.

2. After each health interview was completed, a telephone follow-up interview was conducted (by a different interviewer) with the respondent about the respondent's reaction to the interview experience and the interviewer.

3. When interviewers completed their assignments, they were asked to complete a self-administered questionnaire. This questionnaire included questions about interviewer priorities, interviewer feelings about the job, and some test questions designed to measure some of the interviewers' skills.

Table 7.1

Summary of Training Experiences by Length of Training (in minutes)

	Length of Training Program			
Content of Training:	< 1 Day	2 Days	5 Days	10 Days
General Administration				
Lectures on pay forms, confidentiality, general job procedures	50	75	135	135
General Interviewing Procedures				
Movie	0	90	90	90
Lectures/discussion	120	180	420	420
Demonstrations	55	15	25	25
Supervised practice and exercises	0	105	455	575
*Other interviewer presentations/ discussion/activities	0	0	0	1140
Study Briefing				
lecture on specific question objectives and study procedures	75	165	180	180
TOTAL (minutes)	300	630	1305	2565
(hours)	5	10.5	21.75	42.5

NOTE: Before training began, all interviewers were asked to read a manual and to do exercises related to filling out pay forms and procedures for selecting respondents. Estimated time was 1.5 hours.

*Activities included reading papers on sources of error in surveys and presenting to group; learning how to evaluate interviewer performance using a standard monitoring form; being trained in the elements of coding; and exercises in planning and organizing efficient field trips.

4. One-third of the interviewers were assigned to a pattern of supervision whereby they tape recorded all of their interviews. Coding these interviews provided additional information about how that subset of the interviewers performed.

5. Finally, because each interviewer's sample of addresses was a random subset of the total sample, it was possible to analyze responses from their health interviews and evaluate the extent to which the interviewers affected the answers they obtained.

EFFECT OF TRAINING ON HOW INTERVIEWERS WERE ORIENTED TO THEIR JOBS

One place to begin is how interviewers felt about their training experience. It is not surprising to find that the more lengthy the training experience, the higher the interviewers rated the training as an important source of information (in contrast to the manual, previous work experience, or

Table 7.2

Proportion of Interviewers Saying Their Preparation Was
"Less Than Needed" in Several Areas of Interviewer Skills
by Length of Training Program

	Length of Training Program				
Skill	*< 1 Day*	*2 Days*	*5 Days*	*10 Days*	*p**
a. Planning trips and using time efficiently	30%	46%	23%	7%	.02
b. Explaining the purposes of the study to the respondent	13%	15%	21%	33%	n.s.
c. Gaining respondent cooperation	33%	77%	43%	20%	.02
d. Asking the questions	20%	8%	0%	0%	.04
e. Probing non–directively	54%	70%	14%	7%	.02
f. Meeting question objectives	33%	62%	36%	20%	.14
g. Recording answers	27%	15%	14%	7%	n.s.
h. Handling the interpersonal aspects of the interview	33%	8%	14%	0%	.10
N	15	13	14	15	

NOTE: Probabilities were calculated using chi-squares on a two by two table collapsing the one- and two-day training groups versus the five- and ten-day training groups.

their supervisory feedback). When interviewers were asked to rate the training on a scale from "very good" to "poor," there was a relationship in the expected direction, with those in the 10-day session being significantly more positive, though there was no discernible difference between the ratings of the interviewers in the two shortest programs.

It is also noteworthy that those in the two shortest training programs rated the manual as the most important source of information. In interpreting the findings in this chapter, it is important to keep in mind that those with the least training had an excellent manual and were well supervised. Though their training was short, their opportunities to learn how to properly interview were much greater than would be the case for interviewers who were given a similar amount of training but not given a good manual or similar supervision.

Another question is how well prepared the interviewers felt. Recall that these ratings were made after interviewers had completed their assignments. Table 7.2 shows the results and provides a wealth of interesting information.

In general, it can be seen that the interviewers' ratings of their preparedness were related to how long their training sessions lasted. Not all of the relationships are statistically significant, and only three are perfectly linear, but all but two are generally in the expected direction.

The two relationships that are not in the expected direction have to do with explaining the study and gaining cooperation. In those cases, the least trained interviewers felt as prepared as others. Moreover, interestingly, they turned out to be as successful as those in any other group in enlisting cooperation.

Focusing just on the question-and-answer process and handling the interview, it can also be seen that there is little difference between the five-day and ten-day training groups on any of the dimensions. However, there are two ratings, probing non-directively and meeting question objectives, where the two-day training groups rated themselves much less prepared both than those with more training and, indeed, even than those with less training. On four of the eight ratings in Table 7.2, the people with two days of training rated themselves less prepared than any other group. Although the numbers are small and one deviation could be considered a statistical aberration, this recurring pattern may be meaningful, and we will comment on it again.

Finally, Table 7.2 provides some information about the areas where minimally trained interviewers are most likely to feel unprepared. Clearly the most troublesome area is how to probe, which we have seen is the most critical interviewer skill for a standardized interview. The majority of those interviewers with fewer than five days of training said they did not have enough training in non-directive probing. Three other areas in the table— planning trips and using time efficiently, gaining respondent cooperation, and meeting question objectives—were mentioned by a significant number of interviewers as areas for which they could have used more preparation. These data provide a good outline of where special emphasis in training is most likely to be needed.

A third way one could expect training to affect interviewers is in their perception of priorities, the importance of different aspects of the job. One key difference between those with minimal training and those who had longer training sessions was the amount of training time devoted to the question-and-answer skills, particularly asking questions, probing, and recording. Hence, it would be reasonable to think that the priority of standardization would have come across to them more strongly than to others. When interviewer ratings of their priorities were tabulated, getting accurate, complete answers was rated by all groups to be the highest priority. However, as might be expected, those in longer training programs tended to rate standardization higher than those who had less than one day of training.

Finally, when interviewers were asked how they felt about being an interviewer, there was not a direct relationship to the amount of training received, but once again, those in the two-day training stood out as those who least enjoyed being interviewers.

Table 7.3
Selected Measures of Interviewer Behavior from Coding Taped
Practice Interviews by Length of Training Program

	Length of Training Program			
Percentage of Interviewers *Rated Excellent or Satisfactory*	*< 1 Day*	*2 Days*	*5 Days*	*10 Days*
Reading questions as worded	40%	62%	79%	60%
Probing closed questions	53%	69%	79%	73%
Probing open questions	13%	31%	29%	47%
Recording answers to closed questions	87%	85%	100%	80%
Recording answers to open questions	67%	69%	71%	60%
Non-biasing interpersonal behavior	80%	92%	92%	93%
N	15	13	14	15

NOTE: None of the relationships in this table meets usual standards, on average, for statistical significance.

INTERVIEWING SKILLS

The immediate goal of interviewer training, of course, is to teach interviewers about how to introduce the study, orient respondents, and handle the question-and-answer process. In our research we gathered two kinds of information about how interviewers handled the introduction to the study. First, in their post-study debriefing, the interviewers were asked to answer a series of questions that respondents might ask at the door. These answers were coded for content and accuracy. In general, there was no relationship between the quality of these pencil-and-paper answers and the length of training program to which interviewers were assigned.

The second source of information is from the reinterviews with the respondents. Respondents were asked how well they understood the reasons for the study and how well the interviewer answered their questions. Respondent ratings of how well their questions were answered were unrelated to interviewer training, while the respondents' ratings of how well they understood the purpose of the study were inversely related to the length of training: Those interviewed by interviewers with one day of training rated their understanding slightly higher than average, while those who had interviewers with ten days of training rated their understanding of the purpose of the study significantly lower than average. The results of the paper-and-pencil tests plus the training process itself make it certain that this finding is not due to lack of information on the part of the ten-day interviewers; rather we feel it results from differences in the approach to respondents that the differently trained interviewers adopted.

Additional information comes from the tape recorded practice interviews done right after training was completed. Although none of the individual relationships is statistically significant due to the fact that there were only 15 interviewers in the first group, Table 7.3 shows that those with the least training tended to be rated less than satisfactory at asking questions and probing. It also shows that there was not much difference in interviewing skills after training among the other three training groups.

As noted previously, one-third of the interviewers in each training group were required to tape record all of their interviews during the study, unless a respondent demurred (a relatively rare event) or the equipment malfunctioned (a somewhat more common event). Thus, for those interviewers, we have detailed knowledge of how they carried out the question-and-answer process for most of their respondents. Table 7.4 summarizes these data.

For those interviewers who were tape recorded, the patterns are clear. Those interviewers who had less than one day of training were generally inadequate in the way they carried out the interview. They were significantly worse than those with two or more days of training in almost every respect except recording closed questions. It also can be seen that for most of the skills in these tables, there is not much difference between those with two days of training and those with ten days of training. However, for probing, there was a monotonic relationship between the amount of training interviewers received and how well they were rated at carrying out that aspect of the job. Once again, the data show that probing is the hardest part of the interviewer's job in the question-and-answer process, and that more training pays benefits in the ability to do this.

RESPONDENT PERCEPTIONS OF INTERVIEWERS

Why would we expect training to affect the way interviewers related to respondents? By making interviewers more proficient at their task, and possibly more self-confident in how to handle the interview, they might be rated as more professional and competent. Second, probably a distinctive message of interviewer training is the emphasis on task orientation. Relating personally to respondents is likely to lead to bias and other undesirable things, and it is discouraged. These messages probably are clearer as interviewers have more supervised practice and more extended discussion of the interviewer role.

One of the problems we had in assessing these hypotheses was that respondents were almost universally positive about their interviewers. For

Table 7.4

Selected Measures of Interviewer Behavior from Coding Taped Interviews
by Length of Training Program (supervision level III only)

Interviewer Behaviors from Tape Coding	Length of Training Program				
	< 1 day	2 days	5 days	10 days	p
Average no. questions read incorrectly/interview	21	7	14	6	< .01
Average no. of directive probes/interview	8	5	5	3	< .01
Average no. of times failed to probe inadequate answers/interview	8	6	5	5	< .01
Average no. of inaccurate recording of closed question answers/interview	1	1	1	*	< .05
Average no. of inaccurate recording of open question answers/interview	4	2	2	2	< .01
Average no. of instances of inappropriate feedback/interview	2	*	*	*	< .01
Percentage of interviews rated excellent or satisfactory					
Reading questions as worded	30%	83%	72%	84%	< .01
Probing closed questions	48%	67%	72%	80%	< .01
Probing open questions	16%	44%	52%	69%	< .01
Recording answers to closed questions	88%	88%	89%	93%	n.s.
Recording answers to open questions	55%	80%	67%	83%	< .01
Non-biasing interpersonal behavior	66%	95%	85%	90%	< .01

NOTE: *Less than 0.5 times

**Based on F test; degrees of freedom corrected for intraclass correlation within interviewer scores. Based on about 320 interviews for 20 interviewers, an average of 16 interviews per interviewer.

example, when interviewers were rated on a scale from one to ten on dimensions such as professionalism and friendliness, the average ratings were all in excess of 9. This finding probably reflects both the reluctance of respondents to criticize interviewers as well as a genuine positive response to interviewers.

Regardless of the reasons, there was remarkably little evidence from respondent reports that interviewers with different levels of training behaved differently from an interpersonal perspective. For example, there were no differences in rated friendliness, in professionalism, or in the extent to which respondents thought the interviewers were neutral and did not express their own opinions. Respondents were also asked whether they would characterize

Table 7.5

Respondent Ratings by Length of Training Program

Percentage of Respondents Who Said:	Length of Training Program				
	< 1 Day	2 Days	5 Days	10 Days	p*
Interviewers wanted "exact" answer (not general ideas)	70%	78%	82%	77%	.01
Interviewer did an "excellent job" (cf. very good, good, fair or poor)	64%	57%	57%	55%	.02
N	376	310	357	342	

NOTE: *Chi square test, comparing those with < 1 day with all others combined.

their interviewer as businesslike or as someone who took some time to visit; neither related to the training programs.

There were a few differences, however, that suggest that interviewers with more training were more task oriented, while interviewers with less training were more interpersonally oriented. On the task side, respondents were asked how concerned their interviewers were about the accuracy of the data they obtained and whether their interviewers wanted exact answers or whether "general ideas" were enough. These questions were designed to be measures of the extent to which the interviewer was willing to make demands on the respondent, was willing to communicate expectations for performance. There was a statistically significant relationship in respondent perceptions about whether interviewers wanted exact answers, with those with less than one day of training being least likely to have communicated that (Table 7.5). Moreover, there was a trend in the same direction in the respondents' ratings of how concerned interviewers were about accuracy.

On the interpersonal side, although none of the ratings of friendliness or being businesslike showed a predictable association, those with the least training must have been doing something right, because when respondents rated how good a job the interviewer did overall, those with the least training were rated as having done the best job by respondents. There also was a nearly significant relationship in the same direction with how much respondents said they found the interview "interesting."

These differences are not large, and as noted we have found respondents are not sensitive reporters on interviewers' behaviors. In some cases, for example with respect to how neutral interviewers appeared, respondent ratings did not correspond at all with our coding of appropriate interpersonal behavior when we coded tape recorded interviews. However, we do think there is some evidence that an effect of training is to increase the task orientation and, possibly, reduce the interpersonal orientation of interviewers.

EFFECT OF TRAINING ON DATA QUALITY

In this study, there were two measures of data quality. First, rho, the intraclass correlation, measures the extent to which interviewers can be associated with the answers they obtained. In effect, it is a measure of the extent to which a group of interviewers is standardized. Ideally, the value of the intraclass correlation would be close to zero.

Second, there were 54 questions from the survey where we thought we could predict in which direction, on average, the better and more accurate answers would lie. Our predictions were based either on a social desirability hypothesis, that fewer socially desirable answers would indicate less bias, or on an underreporting hypothesis, that minor events and difficult to recall events will be, on average, underreported. Hence, we calculated for each interviewer how the answers they obtained compared with the overall sample average. We then calculated the extent to which training could be associated with interviewers getting what appeared to be more or less biased answers.

In neither case was there a statistically significant relationship to training. In the case of our measure of bias, there is some tendency for there to be an improvement associated with training. Those with the most training collected data that appeared to be least biased, but the less-than-one day and five-day training groups were essentially equal, so it is difficult to reach a definite conclusion.

With respect to standardization, the data are even more complex. The most standardized data were collected by those interviewers who had two or five days of training. Although the size of the sample did not produce firm statistical significance, it appeared that those with less than one day of training and those with ten days of training both tended to be worse than the two middle groups. There is no question that the ten days of training failed to improve the level of standardization of those interviewers.

CONCLUSION

One clear conclusion from this study is that interviewers need supervised practice in general interviewing skills in order to be adequate interviewers. The program that only used reading, lectures, and a demonstration interview was insufficient. Interviewers with minimal training can handle the interpersonal aspects of enlisting cooperation and relating to respondents as well as anybody else, in part because we do not know how to train interviewers in those skills very well. However, they do not feel prepared to handle the question-and-answer process, and the majority of those interviewers were rated as unsatisfactory when their interviews were tape recorded. Moreover, when we look at the quality of data that they collect, although the results are not crystal clear, there is evidence that, both from the point of view of standardization and bias, the data they collect are not as good as those collected by interviewers who have more training. In a study in Belgium, Billiet and Loosveldt (1988) compared interviewers who had virtually no training with a group who went through a three-day program of training. They, too, find clear differences in the way interviewers handled questions that required probing. It is clear that probing skills are critical to standardized interviewing, that they are the most difficult for interviewers to learn, and that those skills benefit most from training.

The interviewers with two days of training clearly had the basic interviewing skills down. In this program they had more demonstrations, discussed what they saw, and had some time for supervised practice. Those with more training, particularly an entire day of supervised practice, were a little better at probing open-ended questions according to our coding of tape recorded interviews. However, from a data quality point of view, those with two days of training collected data that were as standardized and unbiased as any other group we studied. The one darker note with respect to the two-day training programs is that these interviewers did not feel as well prepared as others. They enjoyed interviewing less than any other group. The situation may be different if interviewers are going to work on the telephone, rather than having to operate as much on their own as do personal household interviewers. However, our data indicate that it would be better for interviewer confidence and morale if they received more than what we offered in the two days of training.

The data from the five-day training groups and particularly the ten-day groups show that too much training can be counter productive. When we designed the ten-day training session, our hypothesis was that the more interviewers knew about the reasons for the decisions they have to make, the more likely they would be to make the right decisions in an interview. We failed to appreciate that interviewers can get tired of being trained. By the time the ten-day trainees were finished with training, they were scoring slightly lower than those with two or five days of training when they conducted a practice interview. Most important, the data they collected were less standardized to a nearly statistically significant degree compared with data from those with two to five days of training. Cannell et al. (1977a) report several experiences where interviewers deteriorated over the course of a study, collecting increasingly poor data. Rather than improving with experience, they burned out and became less interested, sloppy or careless. Although our results are not definitive, they are certainly supportive of the hypothesis that a similar phenomenon occurs when training is protracted.

Based on our data, there is no question that there must be supervised practice as part of an interviewer training. It pays dividends in interviewer skill and data quality. The availability of flexible, low-cost video taping equipment is a particularly valuable aid to training of this type. Interviewers can be videotaped while they are doing practice interviews. The results can be replayed for group discussion, providing an ideal way to share insights.

The exact length of optimal interviewing training will depend on the size of the group, the complexity of the details of the particular kinds of projects on which interviewers will work, and perhaps in part on the kind of supervision they will receive after training. However, on average, a reasonable standard is that two to four days of training in basic interviewing skills, with significant opportunities to practice their skills under supervision, will be optimal in most interviewing settings. However, the value of training also is related to the way interviewers are supervised after they are trained. That is the issue to which we turn in Chapter 8.

8

Interviewer Supervision

Supervision refers to the process of gathering information about how interviewers perform when they are collecting data, evaluating that information, and providing feedback about those evaluations to interviewers. We differentiate between training, which occurs before interviewers actually begin collecting data, and supervision which begins after they start interviewing.

There are five different aspects of an interviewer's work that survey organizations can supervise:

1. how much work they do, which might be simply the number of interviews they take during some period of time or might include other activities as well;
2. how many hours they work;
3. their response rates, the percentage of the respondents assigned to them that they actually succeed in interviewing;
4. the quality of their completed interviews; and
5. the way they handle the interview process and their interaction with the respondent.

INFORMATION FOR SUPERVISION

Survey organizations vary significantly in the way in which they supervise interviewers. Virtually every survey organization keeps track of how many hours interviewers work and how many interviews they do. However, it is not always a straightforward task to interpret the number of dollars or hours per interview as a measure of the efficiency or cost effectiveness of an interviewer. Such an interpretation depends on comparability of assignments. If some interviewers have assignments in which respondents are particularly hard to find or work shifts in a telephone facility in which calls are less likely to yield interviews, these factors, rather than interviewer performance, may account for variations in costs per interview. Moreover, during the course of a study, it may be hard to get a meaningful interim reading on efficiency. Nonetheless, almost all organizations collect information about cost per interview by interviewers and use that information as part of the way in which they evaluate interviewer performance. As important as costs are to any survey organization, of course, they may have little or nothing to do with the quality of data collected.

It also is virtually universal to attend to the rate at which interviewers are successful in enlisting cooperation. If an interviewer is given an assignment of people to contact for which he or she is totally responsible, it is an easy matter to calculate a response rate for each interviewer. Again, evaluation of a response rate should take into account the characteristics of the sample; if one interviewer's sample is easier to reach or more cooperative than another's, it may be hard to reach a firm conclusion about their relative performance.

It also is difficult to monitor response rates on an ongoing basis during a study. How successful an interviewer will be in enlisting cooperation may not be evident until an assignment is nearly completed. Strategies that have interviewers report initial refusals or reluctant respondents on an ongoing basis before an assignment is complete may provide supervisors with some helpful information about interviewers who are having trouble, but such techniques are dependent on interviewer reporting, which is generally imperfect.

When assignments are shared by a group of interviewers, monitoring response rates during a study, or evaluating interviewer effectiveness, is even more difficult. On telephone studies, where the shared approach is the most common, it is particularly difficult to evaluate individual interviewer effectiveness in this respect. Supervisors can keep track of the number of refusals and successful interviews that can be attributed to an interviewer, but it is difficult to know whether a particular interviewer's contacts were representative. Moreover, whether a contact is coded as a "refusal" or something else depends in part on how the interviewer chooses to present the situation. Some interviewers will report a refusal in the same situation that another interviewer will say that they found the respondent busy at the time of contact.

Additionally, most organizations will do some evaluation of how adequately interviewers gather the information they are supposed to and how well they follow the interview protocol. The way organizations do that is to review completed interviews. Most, but by no means all, organizations have some set of procedures for systematically reviewing completed interviews to make sure that interviewers appropriately followed instructions for gathering data, including following contingency patterns, recording answers appropriately, and obtaining answers that meet question objectives.

Organizations differ widely in how much checking they do and in how they deal with problems that they find.

Perhaps the most typical pattern would be to review the first completed interview or two done by an interviewer, and to talk with the interviewer if any serious problems are found. A somewhat more thorough approach is to continue to review a sample of each interviewer's work throughout a survey, and to provide interviewers with written or oral feedback either periodically through the study (which obviously is better in terms of improving performance on that project) or at the end of the study, which at least alerts the interviewer to certain kinds of problems for future studies. An even more intensive strategy is to have someone review every interview to make sure that all necessary data have been collected. Some organizations require interviewers to recontact a household if they have failed to get all the data required. While it would be unusual to have that kind of policy for every single item on a lengthy questionnaire, it is more common for a few key measures that are critical to the survey's goals.

For the purposes of our concerns in this book, namely ensuring the quality of measurement in surveys, all of the above supervisory steps are essentially irrelevant. Little of this has anything to do with the quality of interviewing, the way that the interviewer actually carries out the question-and-answer process. In fact, without special efforts to gather information about the interviewing process, a supervisor cannot review that aspect of the work. By looking at a completed interview schedule, one can derive very little about how the data were collected. If there are open-ended questions that are supposed to be recorded verbatim, one can peruse the answers and identify interviewers who are clearly summarizing or paraphrasing. Many research organizations require interviewers to record the specific probes they use, and if they do that properly, the supervisor can see if appropriate probes are being used. Obviously, this review encompasses a very limited subset of the skills required to be a good standardized interviewer.

Unless the interview process is directly monitored, it is impossible to tell whether or not the interviewer asks questions exactly as worded; one can not monitor the quality of probing, particularly whether directive or non-directive probes are used; a supervisor cannot really tell whether interviewers are exercising discretion in the way they record answers; and a supervisor can not tell anything about the quality of the relationship which has been established between interviewer and respondent.

There are two potential consequences to not supervising the way interviewers interview. First, of course, interviewer problems are not detected and interviewers who can not or will not do the job properly can not be retrained or retired. Second, it fails to communicate to interviewers that standardized interviewing, the way in which they carry out the question-and-answer process, is very important. If, after spending several days in training interviewers in how to conduct standardized interviewing, a research organization does not care enough about standardization to monitor performance, it would be very hard for an interviewer to maintain the goal of standardized interviewing as a priority. Moreover, as we have discussed previously, there are forces, such as a sense that many respondents would prefer a more relaxed, informal interaction, or pressures to be efficient and get interviews over quickly, that push interviewers in the direction of being unstandardized. Therefore, from a management perspective, it seems very important that the question-and-answer process be monitored on a routine basis.

The steps needed to monitor the quality of interviewing obviously differ by whether interviewing is taking place from a central telephone facility or elsewhere, such as in people's homes.

Telephone Monitoring

Most centralized telephone interviewing facilities are equipped with a monitor telephone whereby a supervisor can cut into and out of an interview in progress without being heard or interrupting the interview. Any telephone facility that does not have this capability should acquire it.

Occasional listening to each interviewer by a supervisor will serve to identify interviewers who do not have the idea at all about how to be an interviewer. However, in our view effective supervision requires a more systematic approach. Specifically, we think there are four features of an effective telephone supervision program:

1. Each interviewer is monitored for a complete interview on a regular, frequent basis. By frequent we mean that at least one in ten interviews should be monitored.

2. Monitoring should be done by someone who is specifically trained in how to evaluate interview performance. It is important that when more than one monitor is involved there be training to ensure common standards and expectations.

3. A monitor should be required to fill out a systematic evaluation form about the interviewer's performance for each interview that is monitored. In our experience, if supervisors simply listen and try to note mistakes, they are much more likely to be erratic and inconsistent, and they do not attend to all aspects of interviewer performance. Moreover, they are likely to attend only to the problems, and not consistently identify those things that the interviewer does well. An example of a monitoring form is given in Table 8.1. Cannell and Oksenberg (1988) describe a similar set of procedures.

4. A supervisor should meet with the interviewer immediately after monitoring to go over the form. This ensures timely feedback, when it can be most helpful, and can also make sure that the positive as well as the negative parts of the interviewer's performance are pointed out.

Monitoring Personal Interviewers

The mechanics of gathering information about the question-and-answer process when interviewers are not working out of a central facility are obviously more difficult. For many years, the standard approach to this problem was to have a supervisor accompany an interviewer on an interview or two after training was completed and, perhaps, occasionally thereafter. Such a procedure can succeed at finding out whether or not interviewers can interview, but it obviously gives little information about how they conduct interviews on a routine basis. Moreover, because of the time and expense involved, such observation interviews tend to be extremely rare after initial training is over. Veteran interviewers are seldom observed.

The advent of low cost, portable tape recorders has made it feasible to supervise the question-and-answer process in personal interviews on a more routine basis. Interviewers can be asked to tape record all, or a sample, of the interviews they take, which then can be evaluated by a supervisor. Of course, respondents have to give their permission for an interview to be tape recorded, but in practice this is seldom a problem. Explaining that the tape recording is part of the quality control process is accurate and understandable to respondents, and they seldom have any objections.

We have several practical suggestions for how to manage supervision through tape recording:

1. Interviewers should be asked to tape all of their interviews over some period of time rather than simply choosing one or two of their respondents for tape recording. The facility of the respondent has a good deal to do with the difficulty of the interview. It is easier to be a "good" interviewer with a good respondent. As a supervisor, obviously one wants to see interviewers perform with various kinds of respondents.

2. Assuming that all interviews have been taped, supervisors can then decide how many of the tape recorded interviews they actually want to listen to. There may be practical reasons why tape recording only a sample of an interviewer's work is all that can be done. However, in our experience, the more interviews that are tape recorded, the better.

3. When supervisors do listen to tape recorded interviews, they should use the same kind of systematic form and evaluative procedure as we outlined for telephone monitors. They should be trained in using evaluative scales and

Table 8.1
Monitoring Form

Name: _____

Monitor:____ From intro or Q.____ To Q.____ Feedback date:____ Score:____

A) Introduction: Verified phone number [ ] and is residential [ ]

B) States: Name [ ]   Sponsor [ ]   Purpose [ ]

C) Explains: Confidentiality [ ]   Voluntary [ ]   Can skip Qs [ ]

1. READS questions exactly as written	20 [ ]	ALL CORRECT
Questions incorrectly asked: _____	15 [ ]	1-2 INCORRECT
_____	10 [ ]	3-5 INCORRECT
_____	0 [ ]	MORE THAN 5
2. PROBES nondirectively and appropriately	20 [ ]	ALL CORRECT
Directive or inappropriate (cite questions	15 [ ]	1-2 INCORRECT
and probe) _____	10 [ ]	3-5 INCORRECT
_____	0 [ ]	MORE THAN 4
3. FAILS to probe when necessary	20 [ ]	NEVER
Question number: _____	15 [ ]	ONCE
_____	10 [ ]	2 OR 3 TIMES
_____	0 [ ]	4 OR MORE
4. SKIPS incorrectly _____	20 [ ]	NEVER
Questions: _____	10 [ ]	1 OR 2 WRONG
_____	0 [ ]	3 OR MORE
5. FEEDBACK: inappropriately personal or	20 [ ]	NEVER
evaluative of answers	10 [ ]	1-2 TIMES
Questions/Comments _____	0 [ ]	3+ TIMES
6. TRAINING: Explains R's role, tasks & reasons	20 [ ]	YES—WHEN NEEDED/ WELL
when needed _____		
Comments: _____	10 [ ]	YES—BUT COULD HAVE DONE MORE/BETTER
_____	20 [ ]	NO—NO TRAINING NEEDED
_____	0 [ ]	NO—FAILED TO TRAIN OR DID SO POORLY
7. PACE:	20 [ ]	SLOW
	10 [ ]	MEDIUM
	0 [ ]	FAST

in the standards to be applied. They should do ratings of various aspects of interviewer behavior to be sure they attend to both the positive and negative aspects of the interviewer's performance.

4. One of the biggest challenges is to evaluate tape recorded field interviews

and provide feedback to the interviewers in a timely manner. Otherwise, the interviewers will not be able to remember the circumstances and will benefit less from the feedback. However, even if it is not possible to make these evaluations very timely, the fact that interviews are being monitored will communicate to interviewers that the quality of their interviewing is important.

A STUDY OF THE EFFECT OF MONITORING INTERVIEWERS

The arguments outlined above for the value of systematic monitoring of interviewers have seemed compelling to us for years. Hence, such supervision has been a standard part of our own work. However, there are costs involved in this kind of supervision, and it has not been a standard operating procedure in many other survey organizations. We have been concerned with finding out how much difference such supervision makes and how it affects data quality. The only published study on the topic of which we are aware (Billiet and Loosveldt, 1988) produced some evidence of positive effects. The study described in Chapter 7 on the effect of training on interviewers also included a component that looked at the way different supervision programs affected interviewer behavior and data quality.

It will be recalled that 57 interviewers were assigned to one of four training groups, lasting from one half day to ten days. When training was completed, interviewers were systematically assigned to one of three supervision programs.

All interviewers in the study were scheduled to have one telephone conversation per week with a supervisor. At that time, interviewers received feedback on the quality of work they had done during the previous week. The differences in supervision programs lay in the kinds of feedback interviewers received.

Supervision level one received feedback only about their productivity, their costs, the number of hours they had put in, and their response rates. It was our feeling that the evaluation of those components of interviewer performance was virtually universal, and that many survey organizations provided feedback only on those aspects of interviewers' work.

Supervision level two involved giving feedback on all of the above areas and, in addition, the results of evaluation of a completed interview schedule. Evaluation of a completed schedule focused on whether instructions were followed and recording seemed complete and accurate. Although such evaluation did not touch directly on the question-and-answer process, feedback about these issues would communicate a concern about the data that were being collected, in contrast to supervision level one. In addition, this program of supervision probably replicated the kind of feedback that methodologically rigorous survey organizations routinely give to their personal interviewing staffs.

Supervision level three required interviewers to tape record all of their interviews. At least one tape recorded interview was systematically evaluated each week, and the feedback from the supervisor included evaluation of how the interview was conducted. Also, feedback on issues covered in levels one and two were included.

Ironically, we cannot directly evaluate the impact of these supervisory programs on the way the interviewers carried out the question-and-answer process simply because we lack that information for interviewers assigned to Supervision Levels One and Two. However, we do have information from reinterviews with the respondents and the interviewers' own reports that we can use to evaluate the impact of supervision. In addition, most importantly, we can compare the quality of data that were generated by interviews under each of the supervisory programs.

One additional comment. The presentation of findings about the effect of supervision on interviewers is complicated by the fact that for some critical measures there was an interaction between the amount of training interviewers had had and the effect of supervision. Specifically, when work was supervised through tape recording, it sometimes caused special problems for those with minimal training. These interactions will be noted at the appropriate places in the analyses.

As in the preceding chapter, we will divide the discussion of the effects of supervision into four parts:

1. interviewers' orientation to the job;
2. respondents' reactions;
3. interviewing skills; and
4. resulting data quality.

INTERVIEWER ORIENTATION TO THE JOB

The first question to ask is whether or not interviewers noticed the difference in the content of the feedback they received in the various supervision programs. The answer is clearly "yes." There was the expected monotonic relationship in how highly interviewers rated the feedback they received, with the biggest difference between those who received evaluation only about response rates and costs (level 1) and those who also received feedback about the quality of the interviews they completed (levels 2 and 3).

Across all groups, practice on the job, previous work experience, and training were all rated higher than feedback from supervisors as a source of information about how to interview. Nonetheless, the impact of the supervisory programs was reflected in the ratings of the importance of feedback from supervisors in the expected direction: those in supervision level I rated feedback from supervisors as a relatively less important source of information about how to do the job than interviewers in the other two programs.

One of the main arguments for tape recording interviewers is to communicate to interviewers that the way they handle the question-and-answer process matters. Given the many facets of the interviewer's job, we reasoned that issues such as standardization may drop in priority if they are not directly supervised. As a middle ground, we thought that providing feedback about completed interviews, even though that feedback necessarily cannot address how the data were collected, at least would create a sense of concern about the data that could be important in affecting interviewing performance.

Data related to this issue come from interviewer perceptions of priorities of the Center for Survey Research with respect to interviewer performance. As Table 8.2 shows, interviewers in the three supervisory programs showed markedly different profiles of their perceptions. While all groups thought that obtaining accurate answers was the most important goal at the Center, those who received the level I program of feedback thought that response rates and efficiency were significantly more important to the Center than did interviewers in the other supervisory programs. In contrast, interviewers in supervision levels II and III rated being a standardized interviewer as significantly more important in the priority structure of the Center. Altogether, the data demonstrate very clearly that the kind of feedback interviewers received about their performance affects their perception of what the organization cares about. Although that may not be surprising, these data indicate that the values of the organization are communicated to interviewers in part through the feedback they receive. They are quite consistent with our contention that any aspect of interviewer performance that is not consistently evaluated is unlikely to be considered a priority.

Finally, one might ask how the programs of supervision affected the interviewers' feelings about the job of being an interviewer. It is a common fear that interviewers will not like to be tape recorded and closely monitored. Although there will be some initial complaints from a minority of interviewers, our experience is that they get used to it when it is presented as routine. Our data from the training and supervision study are consistent with our experience; we find little evidence that it had a negative effect on how interviewers responded to their job. Specifically, there was no relationship between the way interviewers were supervised and how they said

Table 8.2

Interviewer Rankings of Importance of Various Goals
to Center Staff by Level of Supervision

Goals	Ranking of Importance to Center (1—Most; 5—Least) Supervision Level		
	I	II	III
Response rate	2.5	3.3	3.0*
Being efficient	2.9	3.2	3.2*
Being standardized	2.6	2.4	2.3*
Obtaining accurate answers	1.5	1.5	1.4
Finishing assignment quickly	4.6	4.7	4.8

NOTE: *Significant differences across the three levels of supervision, $p < .05$, F test.

they felt about being an interviewer. Interviewer ratings of how the study was managed were related to supervision level, but in an odd way. Level 2 was least positive. Level 3 was most positive.

When interviewers specifically rated their supervisory programs their ratings were significantly higher when they were more thoroughly supervised. Moreover, tape recorded interviewers valued their training more than interviewers who were not. We believe that is because training was geared to the question-and-answer process, but only those in level III were actually evaluated on how well they performed in that area; hence, only they actually directly benefited from learning the messages emphasized in training. Overall then, tape recording did not have a negative effect, and in some respects had a clearly positive effect, on the way interviewers rated their experience.

EFFECTS OF TAPE RECORDING ON RESPONDENTS

One could think that tape recording interviews might affect respondents in two different ways. On the one hand, they might react negatively to the interview experience because they do not like to be tape recorded. On the other hand, to the extent that being tape recorded affects interviewers' behavior, respondents may perceive the interview differently.

We examined a variety of respondent reports about their reactions to the interview and the interviewer. For example, we looked at the reports of how important they thought the interview was and how interested they were in it. We also looked at their answers to whether they thought any questions were too personal or whether they had difficulty answering questions completely accurately because the answers were embarrassing. None of these respondent ratings was related at all to whether or not their interviews were tape recorded.

We also studied respondent ratings of the interviewer and how the interviewer behaved. Although we did not believe respondents could give us good information about how interviewers asked questions and probed answers, we were interested that there were no statistically significant differences in their reports of whether interviewers took their time or went quickly, or whether interviewers stuck to the interview or took some time to visit, how friendly interviewers were, or how professional interviewers were. In all of these respects, there were no statistically significant relationships between the presence of tape recorders and respondent ratings.

We also looked at respondent ratings as to how concerned the interviewer was about the accuracy of the respondents' answers, and whether interviewers wanted exact answers or only general ideas. Again, despite the fact that answers from over 1300 respondents were analyzed, so that the reliability of these data is quite high, no consistent relationships appeared with whether or not interviews were tape recorded.

The only statistically significant difference in respondent reports associated with supervision level was how nervous or relaxed interviewers appeared. Interviewers who were tape recorded were rated as being less relaxed by their respondents. Moreover, it is significant that it was those interviewers who had received less than one day of training and who were tape recorded who were most distinctively rated as being nervous.

In summary, there was no evidence from the reinterviews with the respondents of any negative reaction to the tape recording. Of course, any respondent who did not want to be tape recorded was not; it was done only with respondent permission. Nonetheless, fewer than 10% of the respondents refused to be tape recorded. From that perspective, tape recording clearly is a feasible way to exercise quality control on interviewers.

EFFECT OF MONITORING ON INTERVIEWER SKILLS

We noted previously that we were unable to compare the actual question-and-answer process of interviewers who had different programs of supervision because, without tape recording, we did not have data about what actually happened in the interview. However, for the subset of interviewers who were tape recorded, we had some evidence about how systematic feedback influenced interviewer skills over time. Each interviewer's assignment was divided randomly in half. Hence, we were able to compare results from the first and second parts of each interviewer's assignment to see how things changed. For those who were tape recorded, we compared the ratings of interviewing behavior in the first and second half of each interviewer's work.

Three points should be noted in looking at Table 8.3. First, necessarily we are looking at change over a very short period of time. Interviewers only worked for five or six weeks on this study. Hence, we are comparing the first two or three weeks of interviewers' work with their work in the fourth, fifth, and sixth weeks. Second, although interviewers were instructed to tape all of their interviews, only one or two interviews per week were discussed with them. They had one conversation per week with a supervisor about their performance. Hence, interviewers only had a total of three or four feedback sessions with their supervisors. Finally, there was not any real attempt to retrain interviewers; the goal of the supervisory program was to communicate the standards for interviewing and the extent to which interviewers were meeting them.

With those qualifications, it nonetheless is striking that interviewers did not improve their interviewing skills very much over the course of this study. Although the differences observed generally are in the expected direction, basically the ratings in the first half and the second half of interviewers' assignments were, on aggregate, the same. Moreover, when one looks at the data for interviewers with different amounts of training, the same pattern basically emerges. Although those with less than one day of training had very poor interviewing skills to begin with, they did not get any better even when they were tape recorded and received evaluative feedback (Table 8.4). The only real change was in the five-day group, whose performance in the second half of the project rose to the level one would have expected from them.

From these data we conclude that monitoring and feedback alone do not improve interviewing skills. The level of ability displayed by the interviewers at the end of training is the best they are likely to get unless additional retraining steps are taken. Our view is that training which uses supervised practice is the critical step in teaching standardized interviewing skills, while supervision is the critical way to make sure those skills are used.

EFFECTS OF MONITORING ON QUALITY OF DATA

As with our analysis of the impact of training, we used two kinds of measures of the quality of data interviewers collected: *rho*, the intraclass

Table 8.3
Selected Measures of Interviewer Behavior from Coding of Taped Interviews
for First and Second Half of Interviewers' Assignment
(all training groups, supervision level III only)

| | Portion of Assignment | | |
Interviewer Behaviors from Tape Coding	1st Half	2nd Half	p
Average number question read incorrectly/interview	14	12	n.s.
Average number of directive probes/interview	6	5	< .05
Average number of times failed to probe inadequate answers/interview	6	6	n.s.
Average number of inaccurate recording of closed question answers/interview	1	1	n.s.
Average number of inaccurate recording of open question answers/interview	3	3	n.s.
Average number of instances of inappropriate feedback/interview	1	1	n.s.
Percentage of Interviews Rated Excellent or Satisfactory			
Reading questions as worded	63%	70%	n.s.
Probing closed questions	61%	73%	< .03
Probing open questions	42%	48%	n.s.
Recording answers to closed questions	88%	91%	n.s.
Recording answers to open questions	68%	74%	n.s.
Nonbiasing interpersonal behavior	81%	87%	n.s.

correlation, which measures interviewer consistency, and a measure of bias, the extent to which interviewers obtained estimates that were judged to be more or less biased than the average of all interviewers. The data are presented in Table 8.5.

With respect to *rho*, there is a small but clear monotonic improvement associated with the programs of supervision; each of the two more intensive programs of supervision had the effect of reducing intraclass correlations on average. In addition, if one compares only those who were tape recorded with the other interviewers, there is a statistically significant difference in the expected direction (one-tailed test).

In addition, however, in this particular study there was an interaction between the amount of training interviewers received and the role of supervision in reducing the intraclass correlation. Specifically, the more intensive supervision programs were distinctively helpful for interviewers who received very little training and for those who received the most training; there was not much discernible impact in this one study on interviewers who had received two to five days of training.

Table 8.4

Rating of Two Interviewer Behaviors from Coding First and Second Half
of Interviewers' Assignment by Training Program
(supervision level III only)

Percent Rated Excellent or Satisfactory in Reading Questions as Worded

	Portion of Assignment		
Length of Training Program	*1st half*	*2nd Half*	*Net Change*
< 1 day	32%	28%	−4%
2 days	83%	84%	+1
5 days	64%	79%	+15
10 days	85%	83%	−2

Percent Rated Excellent or Satisfactory Probing Open Questions

	Portion of Assignment		
Length of Training Program	*1st Half*	*2nd Half*	*Net Change*
1 day	18%	13%	−5%
2 days	57%	54%	−3
5 days	44%	61%	+17
10 days	70%	69%	−1

With respect to bias, there was a trend in the expected direction, but
there was not a statistically significant positive effect overall of tape recording. Once again there was a significant interaction with training. Those who
received less than one day of training but who were tape recorded obtained
extremely biased data. If those interviewers are left out of the analyses,
the data show a significant positive effect for the value of tape recording
in reducing the bias in survey estimates.

CONCLUSION

We are convinced that the quality of supervision of interviewers is a
critical determinant of how well they do the job and the quality of data they
collect, even though supervision alone will not ensure good interviewing
or good data. A particular surprise to us, though perhaps it should not have
been, is our finding that intensive supervision cannot compensate for inadequate training. If interviewers are not ready to perform well as a result
of their training, evaluation and feedback alone will not make them better.
In fact, we have some evidence that inadequately trained interviewers who
were closely supervised performed worse, not better, than they would if
left on their own, particularly with respect to measures of bias.

Table 8.5

Intraclass Correlations for All Items and Average Standard Score (X1000)
of Questions Judged Likely Subject to Systematic Bias
by Level of Supervision

	Supervision Level		
Quality of Data Indicator	I	II	III
Intraclass correlation	.012	.010	.008*
Standard score (bias) (all training groups)	4	5	20**
Standard score (bias) (excluding those with less than one day of training)	0	4	34***

NOTE: *t = 1.6, Level 3 vs. Level 1, 2, p < .05, 1-tailed test. A lower score means less interviewer effect.
 **t = 1.0, Level 3 vs. Level 1, 2, p not significant. A higher score means less bias.
 ***t = 1.8, Level 3 or Level 1, 2, p < .04, 1-tailed test. A higher score means less bias.

Another insight that has grown into a conviction because of our research, however, is the importance of close supervision for those interviewers who feel confident in their interviewing skills. Although in all cases the data were not statistically significant, the interviewers in our research that had ten days of training, who were thoroughly familiar with how to be good interviewers, but who were not tape recorded collected data that were less standardized than one would have expected; indeed, such interviewers collected data that were less standardized than interviewers who received less training. Also, the interviewers who were tape recorded *and* highly trained were the most standardized. We are convinced that very experienced interviewers, like our interviewers who were perhaps overtrained, feel increasingly free to use their own judgment about how to interview unless they are systematically supervised.

In short, we think careful monitoring of the interviewers' actual performance in the interview does not teach new skills, but it helps ensure that interviewers will use the skills they have. Although we only had data from a single six week study, complementary results have been reported by others. Cannell et al. (1977a), for example, report a steady decline in the validity of hospitalization data collectd by interviewers over a five week study, with each week away from training yielding increasingly worse data. They also report a high negative correlation between the number of interviews an interviewer has to take and the percentage of known hospitalizations reported to those interviewers. In another study, Bradburn and Sudman (1979) reported that experienced interviewers were significantly more casual about the way they worded questions (meaning they misread them more often or added their own words) than new interviewers. In short, although the data are not abundant, when they exist they tend to point in the direction that as interviewers gain more confidence in their skills, they also are likely to get away from some of the behaviors which are important to the collection of good quality data; in short, they become less standardized.

As more and more interviewing is done on the telephone, it is increasingly feasible to have systematic supervision of interviewer performance. In fact, one of the great strengths of the telephone methodology should be the potential to ensure standardized interviewing. Moreover, another great strength of the telephone monitoring system is the potential to give virtually immediate feedback to interviewers.

In addition, we think we have demonstrated that tape recording is a viable and effective way to accomplish positive results when interviews are done in person. The evidence is clear that respondents do not mind, that tape recording does not affect the interview experience from the respondent's point of view. Second, there are clear data from interviewers that when they are monitored, they perceive the increased priority of standardization to the survey organization. Finally, although the impact of more intensive questionnaire review and tape recording does not show up for all training groups on all measures, with the exception of those who receive less than one day of training, there is a pattern of generally positive effects of tape recording on the quality of data that make it clear that it is a valuable adjunct to the total design of a good survey data collection effort.

9

How to Reduce Interviewer-Related Error in Surveys

In this chapter, we attempt to bring together the material presented in the book to provide an integrated summary of how to minimize interviewer-related error.

Interviewers are associated with error in surveys when they are inconsistent in carrying out their part of the question-and-answer process. The answers respondents give in surveys constitute the products of a measurement process. To the extent that interviewers behave inconsistently among themselves, or with different respondents, in ways that affect those answers, it results in less precise and valid measurement. Necessarily the percentage of the variation in answers obtained that can be attributable to the true state of affairs, the true score, that which the researcher is trying to measure, is reduced as a higher proportion of the variation in a set of answers can be attributed to the interviewer.

The staff of interviewers charged with carrying out the data collection in the survey is a collective extension of the researcher. In order to minimize interviewer-related error, the researcher's task is to maximize the extent to which data collection procedures are carried out consistently by all members of the interviewing staff with all their respondents. There are six different ways in which the researcher affects the consistency of interviewing:

1. the wording of the questions interviewers are to ask;
2. the specific instructions or guidelines interviewers are given about how to handle the question-and-answer process;
3. the instructions and procedures interviewers are given for how to set up and maintain the relationship with the respondent;
4. the selection of interviewers;
5. the training of interviewers; and
6. the way interviewers are supervised during the data collection process.

QUESTION DESIGN

We have written elsewhere (Fowler, 1984) that in order for questions to be reliable measures, they must meet at least three standards:

1. the questions must be fully scripted, so that the questions as written fully prepare a respondent to provide the answer;
2. questions mean the same thing to every respondent;
3. the kinds of answers that constitute an appropriate response to the questions are communicated to all respondents.

One critical contribution researchers can make to standardized interviewing is to write questions that meet these standards. When a researcher writes a question that fails one of these standards, it will create a problem for the respondent and the interviewer, and often it is difficult to solve that problem in a standardized way.

It is difficult to write questions that will be perfectly clear and consistently understood by all respondents. However, researchers could do a much better job at this than they do now. The usual procedures for pretesting are wholly inadequate to identify these kinds of question problems. In our experience, senior interviewers are not attentive to the need for slight re-wording of questions during pretests. Pretests often are too small to reliably pick out problems that respondents have with questions. We think that much more attention to questionnaire development in the pretest phase would pay off significantly. Procedures that should be utilized much more than they are now include:

1. One-on-one testing of response tasks and understanding of key terms in a laboratory setting, using the techniques of cognitive psychologists that are only now beginning to come into fashion in the survey research field;
2. greater use of focused discussion groups as a way of getting a better understanding of the way people think about the terms, concepts, and issues that will be addressed in the survey;
3. tape recording and coding of pretest interviews to provide systematic information about questions that are difficult to read as worded, that require clarification, that require repeated probing, or that for other reasons pose difficulties for the respondent and interviewer.

Even these steps will not with certainty produce a perfect questionnaire. However, we believe that many questions, even those used in major surveys with large samples carried out by very professional organizations, could be readily identified as not meeting these three standards. Although the procedures outlined above will not ensure catching all the problems, we are confident that a number of problems could be caught. In our view, no one area would do more to increase the level of standardization of interviewing than the improvement of the design of questions.

INTERVIEWING PROCEDURES

The standard instructions to interviewers about how to carry out the question-and-answer process seem to us to be good ones, assuming that the interview schedule is good. The four standard rules are:

1. Read questions exactly as worded.
2. Probe inadequate answers nondirectively.
3. Record answers without interviewer discretion.
4. Maintain an interpersonally neutral, nonjudgemental relationship with the respondent.

These are fine as far as they go. However, standardization becomes threatened when problems arise that these four principles will not solve.

As noted, the first and best way to deal with such problems is to minimize their occurrence by careful question design. However, when that fails, as it must sometimes, there are pressures on the interviewer to break out of the standardized routine and solve the problem in some idiosyncratic way. In essence, when the question is not clear to respondents or does not fit the respondent's situation, the temptation is for the interviewer to write a question which does. This is particularly tempting when the interviewer does not really have any other tools, or does not know any other options about how to proceed with the interview. The four guidelines above do not tell interviewers how to proceed when the interaction breaks down in one of these ways.

When standardization breaks down because of the way the respondents behave, the correct way for interviewers to proceed is to explain standardized measurement to respondents in a way that allows for the possibility that there will be a problem from time to time. It is not self-evident why a respondent should answer a question when the meaning of the question is not clear, and why that serves the interests of measurement. However, if researchers will train interviewers to train respondents, including teaching interviewers how to explain that very thing, the question-and-answer process can proceed in a standardized way.

THE RELATIONSHIP WITH THE RESPONDENT

Few survey organizations give interviewers much guidance about how to set up the relationship with the respondent, and that largely is because there is not consensus on what is best. In Chapter 4, we examined two aspects of the relationship in some detail: the information respondents are given about the survey and the interviewer's style in relating to the respondent. Our conclusion is that neither of these can be standardized. Respondents differ greatly in the amount of information they bring to an interview and the goals they have, and there is only limited potential to increase the level of respondent information given the kind of methodology that most surveys use. As a result, respondents' information about a survey, their understanding of its purposes, and their own goals for participating are almost certain to vary greatly from respondent to respondent.

With respect to the quality of the interviewer-respondent relationship, while warm professionalism may seem the ideal, there will be great differences in the character of the relationship that interviewers and respondents form. There are genuine limits to the ability of different interviewer-respondent pairs to establish a relationship that meets some ideal model.

While the orientation of the respondent and the character of the relationship to the interviewer cannot be manipulated and controlled, the standards for respondent performance can be made consistent across interviewers and respondents. Cannell and his associates have outlined five different ways to communicate standards to respondents in a consistent way:

1. the pace of the interview;
2. providing a model to respondents;
3. providing consistent instructions to the respondent before and during the interview regarding performance expectations;
4. patterned reinforcement of desired behavior; and
5. asking respondents for a commitment to a specific level of performance.

By incorporating one or several of these strategies into the standard operating procedures for interviewers, researchers can reduce this important source of interviewer and respondent variation and, at the same time, almost certainly improve the quality of their data.

INTERVIEWER SELECTION

There are two kinds of issues with respect to interviewer selection: characteristics which affect the ability of interviewers to handle the measurement process and characteristics which might affect the stimulus situation itself.

From the point of view of interviewer ability, other than good reading and writing skills and a reasonably pleasant personality, we know of no credible selection criteria for distinguishing among potential interviewers.

Interviewers do bring a variety of discernible demographic characteristics to an interview that potentially could affect the interview situation, including age, gender, class, and racial or ethnic background. For most surveys on most topics with most respondents, the demographic characteristics of the interviewers do not affect answers. Moreover, in general, we would say that the procedures outlined previously in this chapter, plus the training and supervision interviewers receive, will overwhelm their demographic characteristics as factors in affecting the amount of interviewer-related error.

However, when questions directly relate to characteristics of interviewers in such a way that respondents would consistently discern (or impose) a preference on the part of interviewers for one set of answers over others, there have been observable interviewer effects on data. For example, interviewers who appear to be Jewish obtain fewer answers that suggest anti-Semitism than interviewers who are not apparently Jewish. Although the results in such situations often are difficult to interpret from the perspective of which answers are best or most accurate, when interviewer demographic characteristics can be associated with answers, it clearly is a source of unreliability and error in the measurement process.

In such cases, researchers may want to consider one of two courses. First, they may choose to use only interviewers who are consistent with respect to a demographic characteristic that they think may affect answers. Second, if all interviewers will not have the same characteristic, the researcher may want to assign representative or comparable samples of respondents to both kinds of interviewers, for example to male and female interviewers, so that the effect of the characteristic (e.g., gender) of the interviewer can be measured and taken into account during analysis.

Overall, however, our most important message is that interviewer selection is probably not an important strategy for minimizing interviewer-related error for most surveys.

INTERVIEWER TRAINING

Talented people do not come naturally to being standardized interviewers. People cannot expect to be acceptable standardized interviewers with less than two or three days of training, that includes supervised practice in the various procedures and problem-solving skills that survey interviewing involves.

Our studies of interviewer training included a group that received about half a day of lectures and demonstrations. In addition, this group had a professional manual to read, a practice interview was reviewed before the start of interviewing, and interviewers were supervised via weekly contacts with an experienced supervisor. Hence, while the training itself was brief, the context in which they were working was thoroughly professional, and the standards for good interviewer performance were clearly communicated to them. Nonetheless, compared even to those who had two days of training, their standardized interviewing skills were generally inadequate. Although they were as good as other interviewers at enlisting cooperation, at establishing a positive relationship with respondents, and at being efficient and productive, tape recordings of their interviews indicated that they were not satisfactory with respect to reading questions, probing nondirectively, recording answers to open-ended questions, and being interpersonally neutral. Moreover, even after they had received feedback on these issues, these skills did not improve noticeably, at least within the six weeks that the study lasted.

The key interviewing skills outlined above are only one part of the process of collecting good data. However, the evidence was quite clear that our minimal training program, the one that lasted about half a day, did not provide adequate training in interviewing skills. If one is going to have a consistent, good quality data collection, interviewers have to receive more training than that.

SUPERVISION

One of our main convictions is that the question-and-answer process must be supervised if one is to have standardized survey interviewing. For telephone surveys, that means a consistent program of monitoring, evaluation, and feedback focused on the way that interviewers handle the question-and-answer process and the relationship with respondents. For interviews that take place in person, that means a program of tape recording, evaluation, and feedback. Our results show very clearly that such a program reduces interviewer-related error and, for interviewers who have received more than minimal training, produces less biased data as well. A program of evaluating completed interviews and providing feedback does help to communicate to interviewers that the way they collect data is important. However, direct monitoring of the question-and-answer process does even more to affect interviewer priorities and emphasize standardization, as well as to improve the quality of data that are actually collected. From our point of view, such monitoring should be a standard part of running a survey operation.

CONCLUSION

The concept of total survey design has come into vogue among methodologists in the past decade or so. By this term, methodologists mean considering all of the facets of a data collection process when making choices about resource allocation in a survey project.

For many years, it seemed as if the design of the sample and the response rate were the only two indicators of a survey's quality. Even today, one will see a footnote that indicates that estimates from a survey have a margin of error of, for example, "plus or minus four percentage points." That footnote is only describing sampling error, the uncertainty of a survey estimate that stems from the fact that the data were collected from only a sample of a population rather than from every individual. That is a readily calculable number: it basically is proportionate to the variation of what is being observed and the size and design of the sample. Such a footnote, however, completely ignores all the many other potential sources of error in survey estimates. Such a footnote implies that sampling error is the only source of error in a survey.

One reason that researchers can treat sampling error as the main or only source of error in surveys is that it is a kind of error which is readily observable and calculable. The other aspect of a survey that has that characteristic is the response rate. However, error stemming from the way the question-and-answer process works, so called response error, generally is not observable and, hence, is often ignored.

In this context, when a researcher is trying to design a survey and decide how to allocate resources, presumably the concern is the minimization of error. Often one reads proposals in which error will be minimized or further reduced by increasing the size of the sample or making the sample design more efficient. Less frequently, but still plausibly, researchers will opt to reduce error by taking steps to increase the expected rate of response. Much too seldom does one see researchers addressing the question of error reduction through the kinds of steps discussed in this book. Yet, there is good reason to think that these steps can have as much or more effect on the quality of survey estimates than increasing sample size. Moreover, in the context of overall survey budgets, most of these steps are comparatively quite inexpensive.

As a concluding exercise, Table 9.1 shows a summary of some of the options available to researchers to improve their estimates, including sample size and various strategies to reduce interviewer-related error. Even based on the data we have available now, it is apparent that steps to reduce interviewer-related error are cost effective ways to improve survey estimates compared with increases in sample size for many estimates. Moreover, almost certainly this table underestimates the potential of these steps to improve survey estimates. For example, designing better survey questions is perhaps the single best way to reduce error that can be attributed to interviewers. In addition, better questions can also improve respondents' ability to answer questions consistently and accurately.

As we noted in Chapter 2, one of the reasons that there is so little attention to the quality of interviewing, and the features of the design of surveys that affect interviewer performance, is that response error and interviewer-related error are not observable without special efforts. Those who do not make special efforts to control interviewer error are distinctively unlikely to make special efforts to measure it. However, as social scientists increasingly are given responsibility for collecting information of importance, it becomes increasingly incumbent upon them to be scientific and to attempt to measure this error in a serious way. It really is not enough to say that the design of questions is an art. Art suggests there are no standards for success other than taste, and that simply is not the case. We have outlined some very concrete standards that can be applied to questions, with the foremost standard being that they can be administered in a standardized, consistent way.

In the same way, being an interviewer is not a matter of feel and taste. There are specific ways to be good and bad at being an interviewer. There are rules that need to be followed. It matters how interviewers interview. We have provided a very large proportion of the rules and standards that interviewers need to follow in order to be good interviewers and to play a key role in a scientific measurement process. Moreover, we have outlined the steps a researcher can take to find out whether or not interviewers are carrying out the measurement process when they are supposed to, and in a way that will produce good measurement.

There are still some gaps in our knowledge. We think we will be able to design better procedures for testing survey questions in the future. We think we may learn even more about the best way to prepare respondents for an interview. We may be able to refine further rules and procedures by which interviewers train respondents. Nonetheless, we believe that we have outlined a set of steps and procedures, well-grounded in empirical literature, that would markedly improve the quality of interviewing and

Table 9.1
Five Ways to Decrease Standard Errors of Estimates

Strategy	Approach	Likely Increased Cost	Effect on Standard Errors
Sample size[1]	Increase effective sample size by about 20%	About a *pro rata* increase in data collection and data reduction costs	Decrease by 10%
Interviewer training[2]	If interviewers receive less than 1 day of basic training, increase by a day or two	Equivalent to about 12 hours of interviewer wages per extra training day per interviewer	Decrease by 10% for the ⅓ of survey items which are most affected by interviewers
Tape supervision[3]	Tape all or a sample of interviews; review one a week per interviewer; provide feedback	About 2 hours/ interviewer per week	Decrease by more than 10% for ⅓ of items most affected by interviewers
Question design[4]	Rewrite questions to reduce need for probing and make administration and reading of questions easier	About twice the length of the interview to tabulate interviewer behavior from taped pretest interviews plus time to rewrite questions	Efficacy not yet demonstrated but data suggest noticeable gains likely
Number of interviews per interviewer[5]	Reduce assignment size by 20% by using 25% more interviewers	Difficult to estimate but certainly less than changing sample size to produce same effect	Decrease by 10% for ⅓ of items most affected by interviewers

NOTE: 1. If a complex sampling design is used rather than simple random sample, this approach may require more than a 20 percent increase in interviews to produce the same effect.
2. Clearly produces direct effects on standard errors if greater than minimal training. However, even more training may also pay off in decreasing bias in data.
3. Probably even greater benefits over time as interviewers deteriorate without taping and feedback. Also, significantly reduces bias for adequately trained interviewers.
4. Likely also to improve respondent reporting.
5. Probably also reduces bias through reduced burn out.

would markedly improve the quality of survey-based estimates. We think the major problem in the field of survey research is less a lack of methodological knowledge about how to proceed than a lack of commitment in the research community to the task of improving the quality of interviewing and survey estimates. We obviously are very hopeful that this book will make a contribution to improving that situation.

REFERENCES

Anderson, B. A., B. D. Silver, and P. Abramson. 1988a. "The Effects of the Race of Interviewer on Race-Related Attitudes of Black Respondents." *Public Opinion Quarterly* 52 (3) 289-324.

Anderson, B. A., B. D. Silver, and P. Abramson. 1988b. "The Effects of Race of the Interviewer on Measures of Electoral Participation by Blacks." *Public Opinion Quarterly* 25 (1) 53-83.

Billiet, J. and G. Loosveldt. 1988. "Interviewer Training and Quality of Responses." *Public Opinion Quarterly* 52 (2) 190-211.

Bradburn, N. A., S. Sudman, et al. 1979. *Improving Interview Method and Questionnaire Design*. San Francisco: Jossey-Bass.

Cannell, C. F. and F. J. Fowler. 1964. "A note on Interviewer Effect in Self-Enumerative Procedures." *American Sociological Review* (29): 276.

Cannell, C. F. and F. J. Fowler. 1965a. "Comparison of Hospitalization Reporting in Three Survey Procedures," *Vital and Health Statistics*, Series 2, (8), Washington, DC: U.S. Government Printing Office.

Cannell, C. F., F. J. Fowler, and K. H. Marquis. 1965b. *Respondents Talk About the National Health Survey Interview*. Survey Research Center. Ann Arbor: University of Michigan. Mimeographed.

Cannell, C. F., F. J. Fowler, and K. H. Marquis. 1965c. *Report on Development of Brochures for H.I.S. Respondents*. Survey Research Center. Ann Arbor: University of Michigan. Unpublished manuscript.

Cannell, C. F., G. Fisher, and Thomas Bakker. 1965d. "Reporting of Hospitalization in the Health Interview Survey," *Vital and Health Statistics*. Series 2 (6). Washington, DC: U.S. Government Printing Office.

Cannell, C. F., F. J. Fowler, and K. H. Marquis. 1968. "The Influence of Interviewer and Respondent Psychological and Behavioral Variables on the Reporting in Household Interviews," *Vital and Health Statistics*, Series 2 (26). Washington, DC: U.S. Government Printing Office.

Cannell, C. F., K. H. Marquis, and A. Laurent. 1977a. "A Summary of Studies." *Vital and Health Statistics*, Series 2 (69). Washington, DC: U.S. Government Printing Office.

Cannell, C. F., L. Oksenberg, and J. M. Converse. 1977b. *Experiments in Interviewing Techniques: Field Experiments in Health Reporting: 1971-1977*. Hyattsville, MD: NCHSR.

Cannell, C. F. et al. 1987. "An Experimental Comparison of Telephone and Personal Health Interview Surveys." *Vital and Health Statistics*, Series 2 (106). Washington, DC: U.S. Government Printing Office.

Cannell, C. F. and L. Oksenberg. 1988. "Observation of Behaviour in Telephone Interviewers." Pp. 475-495 in *Telephone Survey Methodology*, edited by R. Groves et al. New York: John Wiley.

Cohen, A. R. 1958. "Upward Communication in Experimentally Created Hierarchies." *Human Relations* 11: 41-53.

Converse, J. M. and S. Presser. 1986. *Survey questions*. Beverly Hills, CA: Sage.

Converse, J. M. 1987. *Survey Research in the United States*. Berkeley: University of California Press.

Cronbach, L. J. and P. E. Meehl. 1955. "Construct Validity in Psychological Tests." *Psychological Bulletin* 52: 281-302.

DeMaio, T. J., ed. 1983. *Approaches to Developing Questionnaires*. Statistical Policy Working Paper 10. Washington, DC: U.S. Government Policy Office.

Erlich, J. and D. Reisman. 1961. "Age and Authority with Interview." *Public Opinion Quarterly* 25: 39-56.

Fowler, F. J. 1966. *Education, Interaction and Interview Performance*. Ph.D. dissertation, University of Michigan.

Fowler, F. J. 1984. *Survey Research Methods*. Beverly Hills, CA: Sage.

Fowler, F. J. & Mangione, T. W. 1986. *Reducing Interviewer Effects on Health Survey Data*. Washington, DC: National Center for Health Services Research.

Groves, R. M. and R. L. Kahn. 1979 *Surveys by Telephone*. New York: Academic Press.

Groves, R. M. and L. J. Magilavy. 1980. "Estimates of Interviewer Variance in Telephone Surveys." Proceedings of the American Statistical Association, Survey Research Methods Section, 622-627.

Guralk, D. B., ed. 1976. *Webster's New World Dictionary*. Cleveland: Collins and Wood Publishers.

Hensen, R. M. 1973. *Effects of Instructions and Verbal Modelling on Health Information Reporting*. Ann Arbor: Survey Research Center, University of Michigan.

Hyman, H. A., J. Feldman, and C. Stember. 1954. *Interviewing in Social Research*. Chicago: University of Chicago Press.

Jabine, Thomas B., Miron L. Straf, Judith M. Tanor, and Roger Tourangeau, eds. 1984. *Cognitive Aspects of Survey Methodology: Building a Bridge Between Disciplines*. Washington, DC: National Academic Press.

Kahn R., and C. F. Cannell. 1958. *Dynamics of Interviewing*. New York: John Wiley.

Kelman, H. C. 1953. "Compliance, Identification, and Internalization: Three Processes of Attitude Change." *Human Relations* 6: 185-214.

Kish, L. 1962. "Studies of Interviewer Variance for Attitudinal Variables." *Journal of the American Statistical Association* 57: 92-115.

Kish, L. 1965. *Survey Sampling*. New York: Wiley.

Locander, W., S. Sudman, and N. Bradburn. 1976. "An Investigation of Interview Method, Threat and Response Distortion." *Journal of the American Statistical Association*, 71: 269-275.

Lundberg, G. A., et al. 1949. "Attraction Patterns in a University." *Sociometry*. 12: 158-159.

Marquis, K. H., C. F. Cannell, and A. Laurent. 1972. "Reporting Health Events in Households Interviews: Effects of Reinforcement, Question Length, and Reinterviews." *Vital and Health Statistics*, Series 2 (45). Washington, DC: U.S. Government Printing Office.

McKinlay, S. M., D. M. Kipp, P. Johnson, K. Downey, and R. A. Carleton. 1982. "A Field Approach for Obtaining Physiologic Measures in Surveys of General Populations." Proceedings of the fourth conference on health survey research methods. Washington, DC: National Center for Health Services Research, 195-204.

Meisel, A. and H. G. Roth 1983. "Toward Informed Discussion of Informed Consent: A Review and Critique of the Empirical Studies." *Arizona Law Review* 25: 266-341.

Mishler, E. G. 1986. *Research Interviewing*. Cambridge. MA: Harvard University Press.

Newcomb, T. M. 1961. *The Acquaintance Process*. New York: Holt, Rinehart, & Winston.

Payne, S. L. 1951. *The Art of Asking Questions*. Princeton, NJ: Princeton University Press.

Robinson, D., and S. Rohde. 1946. "Two Experiments with an Anti-Semitism Poll." *Journal of Abnormal Social Psychology* 41: 136-144.

Sanders, Barkev S. 1962. *A Health Study in Kit Carson County*. Public Health Service Publication, No. 844. Washington, DC: U.S. Government Printing Office.

Schuman, H. and J. M. Converse. 1971. "The Effects of Black and White Interviewers on Black Responses in 1968." *Public Opinion Quarterly* 35: 44-68.

Schuman, H. and S. Presser. 1981. *Questions and Answers in Attitude Surveys*. New York: Academic Press.

Stokes, S. L. 1986a. "Estimation of Interviewer Effects in Complex Surveys with Application to Random Digit Dialing." Proceedings Annual Research Conference, Bureau of the Census, 2: 21-31.

Stokes, S. L. 1986b. "Estimating Interview Variance for Dichotomous Items Using a Latent Variable Model." *Proceedings* of the Meeting of the American Statistical Assocation, Survey Research Section, 278-280.

Stokes, S. L. and M. Yeh. 1988. "Searching for Causes of Interviewer Effects in Telephone Surveys." Pp. 357-373 in *Telephone Survey Methodology*, edited by R. Groves et al. New York: John Wiley.

Sudman, S. and N. M. Bradburn. 1974. *Response Effects in Surveys: A Review and Analysis*. Chicago, Aldine.

Sudman, S., N. M. Bradburn, E. Blair, and C. Stocking. 1977. "Modest Expectations: The Effects of Interviewers' Prior Expectations on Responses." *Sociological Methods and Research* 6: 177-182.

Weiss, C. H. 1968. "Validity of Welfare Mothers' Interview Responses." *Public Opinion Quarterly* 32: 622-633.

INDEX

ABOUT THE AUTHORS

Floyd J. Fowler, Jr. received a Ph.D. in social psychology from the University of Michigan in 1966. While there he worked on several studies of the sources of error in the National Health Interview Survey. Since then Dr. Fowler has devoted his professional career to learning about, improving, and applying survey methodology. He has been principal investigator for major survey studies of local population trends, attitudes toward local government and services, gambling law enforcement, racial tensions, fear of crime, Jewish identification, and the needs of the elderly. He has provided methodological assistance on well over 100 survey projects, covering most of the substantive policy areas to which survey research is applied. Dr. Fowler has taught survey research methods at the Harvard School of Public Health and elsewhere. For 14 years he has been the Director at the Center for Survey Research at the University of Massachusetts–Boston.

Thomas W. Mangione received his Ph.D. in Organizational Psychology from the University of Michigan in 1973. Since that time he has worked at the Center for Survey Research at the University of Massachusetts–Boston. He has been involved in over 100 survey studies on a variety of topics including alcohol use, drug use, gambling, crime and fear of crime, drunk driving, seat belt usage, work related stress, mental health, and AIDS knowledge and behaviors that put people at risk of AIDS. Through these studies he has gained an appreciation of the difficult task that interviewers face as they try to implement standardized survey procedures. He has conducted research on the quality of data that is collected through survey methods. In particular, he has done research comparing the quality of data which results when asking sensitive questions using a variety of data collection methods. He has also had a long standing interest in the role that interviewing procedures and behaviors may have on the quality of data that is obtained.

Dr. Mangione is currently a Senior Research Fellow at the Center for Survey Research. During his 16 year tenure there he has served as Associate Director and Director of the Center. Dr. Mangione has taught survey research methods classes at both Harvard University and Boston University.